Emotional Disorders & Learning Disabilities in the Elementary Classroom

Jean Cheng Gorman

Emotional Disorders & Learning Disabilities in the Elementary Classroom

Interactions and Interventions

CORWIN PRESS, INC.
A Sage Publications Company
Thousand Oaks, California

For information:

Corwin Press, Inc.
A Sage Publications Company
2455 Teller Road
Thousand Oaks, California 91320
E-mail: order@corwinpress.com

Sage Publications Ltd.
6 Bonhill Street
London EC2A 4PU
United Kingdom

Sage Publications India Pvt. Ltd.
M-32 Market
Greater Kailash I
New Delhi 110 048 India

Printed in the United States of America

Library of Congress Cataloging-in-Publication Data

Gorman, Jean Cheng.
    Emotional disorders & learning disabilities in the elementary classroom: Interactions and interventions / by Jean Cheng Gorman.
        p.   cm.
    Includes bibliographical references and index.
    ISBN 0-7619-7619-1 (cloth: alk. paper)
    ISBN 0-7619-7620-5 (pbk.: alk. paper)
    1. Learning disabled children—Education (Elementary)   2. Emotional problems of children.   3. Behavior disorders in children.   I. Title.
    LC4704.73 .G67   2001
    371.9'0472—dc21   00-012350

This book is printed on acid-free paper.

01   02   03   04   05   06   07   7   6   5   4   3   2   1

Acquisitions Editor:	Robb Clouse
Corwin Editorial Assistant:	Kylee Liegl
Production Editor:	Nevair Kabakian
Editorial Assistant:	Cindy Bear
Typesetter/Designer:	Lynn Miyata
Cover Designer:	Tracy E. Miller

CONTENTS

CLASSROOM INTERVENTIONS

PREFACE

My greatest problem in my childhood is now my greatest asset. I'm trying to tell the kids today that Creation gave us all problems for a purpose, and that your biggest problems contain a source of strength to not only step over those problems, but all our other problems as well.

—John Larkin, "Scatman John"
Award-winning jazz pianist and scat
singer, regarding his stuttering disorder
(Oliver, 1999)

Kathy is about to begin her first year of teaching. She has been assigned a second-grade classroom in an inner-city school and expects to have 34 students. John has been a sixth-grade teacher for 15 years in a wealthy suburban neighborhood and is looking forward to using the technology grant he received from the school district this year. Despite their different environments, both teachers will be expected to teach students with learning disabilities and those with emotional disorders. As inclusion becomes more and more of a reality for general education teachers, the concern is not whether regular education teachers can learn how to teach children with learning and emotional disorders, but that a lack of time, insufficient resources, and competing responsibilities may result in the needs of such children being inadequately addressed. The purpose of this book is to serve as a resource for all teachers who are presented with the challenge of addressing the multiple needs—academic, emotional, and social—of children with learning and emotional problems.

Over the past 10 years, the number of children identified as having learning disabilities has increased by 38% (U.S. Department of Education, 2000), though overall population growth has only increased by 6% (McLeskey, Henry, & Hodges, 1998). A decade ago, these children were primarily taught in separate classrooms (McLeskey, Henry, & Axelrod, 1999), but currently, the majority are being educated in general education classrooms, with 43% receiving pull-out services for less than 21% of the school day (U.S. Department of Education,

2000). The number of students identified as having emotional disturbances is far less than those with learning disabilities. However, it is still the fourth largest category of children served under the Individuals with Disabilities Education Act (IDEA) (U.S. Department of Education, 2000). The actual incidence of children with emotional disturbance may be even higher, given the tendency toward underdiagnosis of childhood psychiatric disorders.

Understandably, many teachers have been apprehensive about including students with disabilities in regular education classes. Some, like Meredith, a fifth-grade teacher, feels that such children "are more work for me, as if I didn't have enough to do already." Others wonder whether they will be able to successfully teach children with significant disabilities, or are concerned that the special needs of these students will dominate their classes. Parents have also raised concerns that their children will receive inadequate help in regular education classrooms. Their worries are supported by research indicating that often only minor modifications, such as preferential seating, are made in the general educational classroom rather than major instructional modifications (Baker & Zigmond, 1990). Not surprisingly, teachers with less positive attitudes toward inclusion tend to use fewer effective instructional strategies (Bender, Vail, & Scott, 1995).

You will be more confident about inclusion when you are equipped with knowledge and skills to deal with learning and emotional problems. This book is unique because it focuses on the interaction of learning and emotional functioning. Understanding how learning problems affect emotional well-being (and vice versa) is crucial to focusing on the whole child, rather than on the disorder or disability. This book does not intend to give elementary school teachers all the answers to teaching children with learning disabilities and emotional disorders. It is intended to help you successfully address learning disabilities and emotional problems in the classroom by providing a base of knowledge and practical interventions you can integrate into your daily routine. This book strives to help you be more purposeful in helping children with learning and emotional problems—and more effective.

Throughout this book, you will see a light bulb icon in the margin whenever interventions are discussed. Some activities are also supplemented with reproducibles you will find at the end of the chapter. The Classroom Interventions Table of Contents refers you to all the activities, interventions, and reproducibles presented in this book. Ideally, they will inspire you to develop other activities tailored to the specific needs of your students. Certainly, these interventions are not a panacea for addressing the complex and in-depth needs of children with learning and emotional disorders, nor are they meant to take the place of formal assistance (i.e., intensive phonics instruction). The interventions in this book should be used to supplement programmed instruction. Although it is unlikely that you will single-handedly eradicate learning disabilities and emotional problems, you are a very important part of the equation. Your efforts and actions have tremendous influence.

Accordingly, this book begins with issues of teachers' well-being and the prevention of burnout, because as teachers, you are faced with multiple demands on your time and energy. It is important not to become overwhelmed by these competing pressures. Although this book will help you to make the most of your efforts, do not overlook the multiple sources of assistance available to you. Collaborating with other professionals, such as reading specialists, school psychologists, speech therapists, and so forth, is good for both you and your students. Additional resources for further learning and intervention are also provided at the end of the book.

Part I consists of Chapters 1 and 2 and provides an overview of common learning disabilities and emotional problems that you may encounter. These chapters ground you in research and contain worksheets to alert you to the possible existence of learning and emotional disorders in your students. These chapters will not make you an expert on learning disabilities or emotional disorders. However, they will make you more familiar with the types of issues you may encounter, so that you will know when to intervene and also when to get help from others. Case studies in these chapters may help you recognize similar problems in your students.

Part II contains chapters that propose five possible interactions between learning disabilities and emotional disorders. Although a great deal of information is also presented, the focus is on classroom experiences, since intervening at an early age can have a significant impact on a child's life outcomes. Chapter 3 discusses the social/emotional development and functioning of children with learning disabilities. Case illustrations provide portraits of how learning disabilities can affect a child's emotional health and social relationships. Children who have learning disabilities and are coping well may require only cognitive remedial support, but children who are experiencing significant emotional consequences need special assistance. Tangible steps you can take to prevent or diminish these problems are featured throughout the chapter.

Chapter 4 describes how emotional problems can hide learning disabilities. Some emotional problems, such as aggression, can overshadow learning problems. Failing to treat such learning disabilities, even if help is given for the emotional problems, is problematic because children need solid academic skills for future success. Behavioral analysis worksheets and other aids help you distinguish between the emotional disorders and learning disabilities. Reproducibles that help you deal with emotional problems in your students are also provided.

Chapter 5 presents information on how learning disabilities can actually magnify preexisting emotional problems. Specific teaching aids and other classroom interventions are offered to help minimize these problems. Chapter 6 details the reverse process: when students' academic progress is hindered by their emotional struggles. This chapter also provides suggestions on ways to empower children to focus on overcoming their learning problems.

Chapter 7 focuses on how teachers can facilitate students' academic performance by building their social and emotional functioning. Activities for establishing a positive supportive climate in the classroom and fostering social and emotional competence are presented.

Teaching elementary school-aged children is already demanding, without feeling that you have an additional "burden" of dealing with learning disabilities and emotional disorders. With the all too common realities of too many students in too small a space with too little time and resources, it would be easy to avoid things that require extra effort. However, if you have a solid foundation of knowledge about learning disabilities and emotional disorders and incorporate some of the activities included in this book, helping children overcome learning and emotional disorders will feel natural rather than an added responsibility. Over time, what seemed so complicated and time-consuming in the beginning will become routine. The reward is knowing you have changed a child's life.

ACKNOWLEDGMENTS

My deepest gratitude to J. C. who is my inspiration; and to my parents, who taught me the value of education; much appreciation for my husband for his unwavering confidence in me; many thanks to my sister, Patty, for her support and practical help during the writing of this book; thanks also to Robb Clouse and the staff at Corwin Press who made this all possible.

The contributions of the following reviewers are gratefully acknowledged:

Nettye Brazil
Department of Special Education, University of Louisville
Louisville, KY

Merle Burbridge
Ramona Elementary School
Hemet, CA

Douglas Cheney
Department of Special Education, University of Washington
Seattle, WA

Christopher Kliewer
Department of Special Education, University of Northern Iowa
Cedar Falls, IA

Dave Lochner
Levy Middle School
Syracuse, NY

James McLeskey
Department of Special Education, University of Florida
Gainesville, FL

Joyce Mounsteven
Special Education Department, Toronto District School Board
Toronto, ON

Cindy Munson
Travis Middle School
Amarillo, TX

Rex Shahriari
Department of Education, Central College
Pella, IA

Jolinda Simes
Career-In-Teaching
Minneapolis, MN

Joseph Staub
Thomas Star King Middle School
Los Angeles, CA

Judy Winn
Department of Exceptional Education, University of Wisconsin-Milwaukee
Milwaukee, WI

ABOUT THE AUTHOR

*J*ean Cheng Gorman, PsyD, is a licensed psychologist. In addition to her research on children's emotional health and learning disabilities, she has also published journal articles on Chinese methods of parenting and on culturally sensitive parenting programs. Her other interests include early childhood development (birth to 3 years of age) and the educational needs of children with chronic illness. She studied elementary education and earned her undergraduate degree in psychology at Brown University. She taught in urban and suburban elementary schools before obtaining her doctorate in Child and School Psychology from New York University. She lives with her husband and daughter in California.

To Anna

INTRODUCTION

It is important, as a teacher . . . to "teach" students
how to be their own advocates. . . . When they learn
of their IEP rights, they are empowered and sense,
sometimes for the first time, that they are
not losers or rejects, but valued individuals.

—Anne N. Lin
RSP teacher
12 years of teaching experience
Manhattan Beach, California

The intent of this book is to equip you with information and interventions to help children overcome learning, emotional, and social/behavioral problems that interfere with their growth in the elementary school years. You will be exposed to a great deal of information, research, ideas, and activities. Before you begin, take a few moments to consider some thoughts.

STUDENTS' VIEWS ON LEARNING DISABILITIES

Students have a lot to say about what kinds of interventions they find helpful. For example, studies have found that students with learning disabilities prefer working in small groups of peers or in pairs (Elbaum, Schumm, & Vaughn, 1997; Klingner, Vaughn, Schumm, Cohen, & Forgan, 1998). In part, this may be because they value being able to both receive AND provide assistance. They recognize that instructional adaptations for special needs (e.g., additional work time) are positive (Klingner & Vaughn, 1999; Vaughn, Schumm, Niarhos, & Gordon, 1993), but they do not want to be treated significantly differently, such as by receiving different homework assignments than their peers (Bryan & Nelson, 1994). Furthermore,

> students with learning disabilities want to be involved in the same activities, read the same books, have the same homework, be judged with the same grading criteria, and be part of the same groups as their classmates. . . . [At the same time, they] recognize that not all students learn in the same way or at the same speed. Thus students . . . value teachers who slow instruction down when needed, explain concepts and assignments clearly, and teach the same material in different ways so that everyone can learn. (Klingner & Vaughn, 1999, p. 35).

Your students can tell you what they find most helpful and what they find undesirable. Soliciting and listening to their feedback about your intervention efforts can save you a great deal of time and heartache. Although the information and interventions presented in this book are applicable to the general category of students with learning and/or emotional disorders, each child is unique and will respond differently. Finding what works for your individual student is a challenge but yields great rewards.

A HEALTHY VIEW OF LEARNING AND EMOTIONAL PROBLEMS

As educators, it is natural for you to think of learning and academic achievement as being all-important. After all, it is what you are trained to do—teach children. It is easy to slip into thinking that their cognitive development is your only concern and, as a result, become impatient or intolerant of emotional problems that seem to "get in the way." Remember that a child is much more than what he or she is learning in the classroom. Because we only see a portion of the child's life (and thus an incomplete picture of the child), we have to be careful not to reduce a child down to his or her learning and/or emotional problem(s).

SENSITIVITY TO STIGMATIZATION

Even the best of intentions can result in stigmatizing a child. Overzealousness, too much attention, too narrow a focus on problem areas, and too much "understanding" can, in fact, backfire. Fellow students may be sensitive to what they perceive as unfair special treatment (Vaughn, Schumm, Klingner, & Saumell, 1995). In addition, we may try too hard to accommodate a student with learning or emotional disorders, unwittingly stripping them of the responsibility and control we are trying to foster. That student then becomes labeled, in effect, as incapable and always in need of assistance. Remember that "learning disabled" refers to a specific type of struggle, not to an overall lack of ability, and that childhood "emotional disorders" most often reflect problems in adjustment, not psychopathology. Be sensitive to the impact of your interventions. If they seem to be too overwhelming to the child (e.g., she withdraws or resists your efforts), step back and allow the child to pace you.

Learning disabilities and emotional problems should not be used as excuses for failure and avoidance of negative consequences. Overall, teachers tend to hold greater expectations for future failure for children with learning disabilities than for their nondisabled peers (Clark, 1997). Doing so only conveys the message that there is little hope for change and that very little should be expected from the individual. However, acknowledging, understanding, and accommodating students' learning, emotional, and social disorders convey a respectful attitude toward personal limitations that does not promote helplessness. If you have an attitude of hopeful expectation and are actively involved in students' learning processes, you can have a significant effect on raising student academic achievement (Brophy, 1986).

BEING REALISTIC

Ideally, intervening with a child with significant learning and/or emotional problems should be a natural part of your treatment of each student in your class as unique. It is unreasonable to assume that you can adjust every lesson and class activity to meet the individual needs of every student. Making efforts to accommodate the special needs of your students whenever possible, and asking for help along the way, is much more realistic. You can strive to convey to your students an attitude that recognizes and accepts people for who they are—faults and all—and encourage them to strive for personal improvement. You are the most effective vehicle for this message—how you treat yourself and your own limitations conveys a great deal to your students. Being intolerant of criticism or student complaints, never apologizing for your mistakes, and denying any difficulty will make it hard to teach your students to acknowledge and overcome their own personal areas of struggle.

DEALING WITH FRUSTRATION

Sometimes, try as you might, nothing seems to work. Even things that were "guaranteed" to work did not. Unfortunately, your frustration and anger may result in an "inflexible approach to the child which will lessen the teacher's effectiveness" (Abrams, 1986, p. 194). Should you discover that, despite all of your various efforts, you are only becoming increasingly frustrated and discouraged, it is time to renew your perspective. Remember that you are not alone in your efforts to help, and that your fatigue is probably shared by other significant adults in the child's life. Not only may this give you a better working relationship with the child's parents, but you are likely to have more compassion and understanding toward the child. A child who engenders such difficulty for others is often a very lonely child.

AVOID BURNOUT

This brings us to the topic of overcoming a specific type of emotional problem in the classroom—the teacher's emotional state. Being a conscientious, energetic, innovative teacher means you recognize the tremendous importance of your job and are constantly trying to improve your skills to benefit your students. However, trying to do too much can lead to fatigue and discouragement, which helps neither you nor your students. It is imperative to guard against burnout, which occurs when you have completely depleted and exhausted yourself. Consider the following signs of burnout:

- Irritability
- You dread going to work
- Apathy
- Feeling like nothing is effective
- Excessive fatigue
- Impatience and anger toward students
- Feeling too stressed out to enjoy anything
- Reliance on alcohol/drugs to relax or cope
- Physical discomfort

If these signs begin to characterize you, take steps to care for yourself. Nearly one in six teachers would not choose teaching as a career if they could start over again (Borg, Riding, & Falzon, 1991). This remorse often stems from repeated discouragement and fatigue.

Don't give up in your efforts to help, but recognize your own limitations and seek support when you need it. Take time to look after yourself and to reward yourself for success and effort. Remember—it's not your responsibility, or even within your power, to solve or cure everything for everyone. You are, after all, only human.

NOW WHAT?

If you read this book and think to yourself, "There isn't anything earth-shattering in this book; I already know it all"—wonderful. That means you're probably very aware of issues related to emotional well-being and learning disabilities and are very attuned to your students' needs. Your teaching style and classroom likely already incorporate many effective interventions. If this is the case, use this book as a way of recognizing your efforts and teaching accomplishments. Perhaps it will also encourage you to add to your existing repertoire.

On the other hand, perhaps you'll find yourself thinking, "I don't have time for all this!" Remember that the activities that deal with emotional health also reinforce language and other cognitive skills, and that the learning disability interventions build basic academic skills as well as promote social skills. You're accomplishing instructional goals and, at the same time, nurturing your students, though the methods may seem a bit unconventional. As you read, if you find yourself sighing with despair, take heart. As a teacher of young children, you are already fulfilling multiple roles. Get help by enlisting the assistance of your colleagues and/or contacting the resources at the end of this book so you're not overwhelmed.

Most of you will probably experience something in between these responses throughout the reading of this book. Vacillating between feeling competent and feeling inadequate is a good sign that you are open to growing as a teacher. You have personal gifts for teaching and helping children that led you to becoming an educator. Children's lives are better because of you.

PART I

Overview of Learning Disabilities and Emotional Disorders

1
COMMON LEARNING DISABILITIES

*R*eferrals for Edgar to be tested for learning difficulties
had been made in both first and second grade,
but his mother did not want testing done. . . .
By January [of third grade], she became concerned,
because her first grade son was now reading
and writing better than Edgar was.

—Sarah Ascheman
Third-grade teacher
2 years of teaching experience
Culver City, California

As teachers, you have the noble task of introducing new concepts to children, making the unfamiliar familiar and the incomprehensible understandable. All children have difficulties mastering new material at some point. However, for most children, these problems are transient and do not fit any consistent pattern. For others, learning is a greater challenge because of deficits in core areas such as language, mathematics, and reasoning.

The term *learning disabilities* is a broad term that has been used to encompass problems with language, mathematics, and writing; visual and perceptual problems; and attention or behavior problems. But just what constitutes a learning disability? Some researchers focus on identifying distinct neuropsychological profiles (see Ward, Ward, Glutting, & Hatt, 1999), attempting to find a very scientific or medical definition. Others, such as social constructivists, suggest that the term is inappropriate and inadequate for describing the learning processes of students, because it fails to take into account the "whole child" in an authentic context (see O'Shea, O'Shea, & Algozzine, 1998).

Most educators define learning disabilities according to federal law. The U.S. Office of Education and Public Law 101-476 (Individuals with Disabilities Education Act) defines "specific learning disabilities" as

> a disorder in one or more of the basic psychological processes involved in understanding or in using language, spoken or written, which may manifest itself in imperfect ability to listen, think, speak, read, write, spell, or to do mathematical calculations. The term includes such conditions as perceptual handicaps, brain injury, minimal brain dysfunction, dyslexia, and developmental aphasia. The term does not include children who have learning disabilities which are primarily the result of visual, hearing or motor handicaps, or mental retardation, or emotional disturbance, or of environmental, cultural, or economic disadvantage. (U.S. Office of Education, 1977, p. 65083)

Although debate over operationalizing this definition continues, a significant discrepancy between achievement and intellectual ability (as measured by performance on achievement and intelligence tests) is used by many states to identify a student as learning disabled (Mercer, King-Sears, & Mercer, 1990). Some consider at least 2 standard deviations between intellectual ability and academic functioning to be significant. This means that a child whose IQ is 100 (average) would need to score below the 9th percentile for his or her age on diagnostic tests in order to be diagnosed with a learning disability. Most children with learning disabilities have average intelligence but achieve far below what is expected for their age and intelligence (Smith & Luckasson, 1995). True learning disabilities are thought to be lifelong disorders (Schonhaut & Satz, 1983).

This chapter presents a brief overview of learning disorders that may be encountered in the classroom. It is certainly not an exhaustive presentation of learning disabilities, and other works, such as introductory textbooks by Lerner (1993) and O'Shea et al. (1998), present more in-depth information. Although this chapter describes discrete areas of learning disabilities, it is important to bear in mind that many children may have elements of several areas of difficulty that do not fall neatly into the categories featured here. At the same time, several learning problems can stem from a global learning disability, as in the second case study.

READING

Reading disabilities are likely what comes to mind when you think of learning disabilities. Problems with reading can involve many areas, including word recognition and comprehension, oral reading fluency, and reading comprehension (O'Shea et al., 1998). Within each of these areas, numerous skills are needed to successfully read. For example, comprehending a passage involves noting important details, identifying the main idea, tracking a sequence of events or steps, drawing inferences and conclusions, organizing ideas, and applying what is read (Lerner, 1993). Students may have difficulty in any of these higher-order skill areas, although their basic reading skills are intact.

The term *dyslexia* has often been used to refer to reading disabilities, and is a familiar term for many people. Some have overused it to describe all problems with reading and writing or have misunderstood it to be a problem with letter reversals (e.g., writing a "b" instead of a "d"). Others believe the term is obsolete and does not reflect more holistic concepts in language (Myers & Hammill, 1990). Still others say that dyslexia is a highly specific disability, partly genetic (Pennington, 1991), likely based in neurological (brain) abnormalities (Bakker, 1992), and does not apply to all children with language-based learning problems.

Despite the controversy, as a type of reading disability, dyslexia is well researched and, relative to other learning disability subtypes, well understood. The core problem area is in phonological processing (Shaywitz, 1996). There are a total of 44 phonemes in the English language. Different combinations of these small sound units make up words. For example, "kuh," "aah," and "tuh" can be combined to form the word *cat*. A child with dyslexia may have trouble distinguishing between phonemes when they are put together. Alternatively, a child may struggle to combine phonemes into words when writing. Reading becomes a chore because of difficulty identifying the sound units that make up the words. Spelling and writing are challenging for the same reason. Decoding exercises and identifying the number of syllables in a word are exceptionally difficult for children with dyslexia.

Recent neuroscience research raises the possibility that people with dyslexia also have an underlying processing speed deficit in addition to their phonological difficulties (Azar, 2000). It may be that people with dyslexia process sounds more slowly than average, making it difficult to distinguish phonemes. This provides additional explanation for why people with dyslexia have problems with reading and spoken language, which are commonly very rapid activities.

Children who are dyslexic may not have problems with speech, but may struggle with interpreting what they hear. For instance, because of their phonological processing problems, they may not be able to tell the word *pat* from *bat*. As a result, children with dyslexia may be viewed as "normal" with the exception of being a "poor reader," a "bad listener," or "inattentive." These children may also be attributed with emotional problems, such as "lack of motivation," because their language processing difficulties may not be obvious. As a result, it is possible for a student with significant dyslexia to be undiagnosed until late in elementary school or even beyond, such as with Brianne in the following case study. In the early school years, "subjects" are based on acquiring learning skills such as reading. In the upper grades, "subjects" become more content-focused (e.g., history or science lessons), and the ability to read is taken for granted.

Consequently, early identification of dyslexia is particularly important, since adequate reading skills are the basis for all other learning (Hurford, Schaug, Bunce, Blaich, & Moore, 1994).

Signs of a Reading Disorder, found at the end of this chapter, may help you identify whether a child needs further evaluation for a learning disability.

✧ CASE STUDY: The Child With Dyslexia

It was mid-November, and Brianne was still struggling to adjust to her fourth-grade class—at least, that was what her teacher thought. She attributed Brianne's moodiness, inconsistent performance, and low achievement to needing more time to become accustomed to the demands of a fourth-grade classroom. Actually, she was giving her the benefit of the doubt, because Brianne was such a quiet, manageable student. In truth, she suspected attention-deficit/hyperactivity disorder (ADHD). How else could she explain the fact that Brianne could get 90% on her spelling test one week and 20% on the next? Reading seemed to be a chore for her, but that was probably because she was distractible and couldn't (or wouldn't) concentrate for the longest lesson of the day. Besides, she always did well in subjects she was interested in, like math. Her memory also seemed to be poor, since she often couldn't remember directions and needed to have them repeated several times. Her teacher reasoned that this was probably because she "wasn't paying attention in the first place."

Brianne's mother was increasingly frustrated and concerned—her daughter was beginning to hate school. Despite her persistent efforts to help her at home, Brianne was falling further and further behind. At her wits' end, she took Brianne to a private psychologist for counseling. Instead, the psychologist diagnosed Brianne's dyslexia and facilitated school interventions.

In this case, Brianne's teacher accurately discerned areas of Brianne's difficulty, yet she misattributed them to ADHD. Brianne's distractibility and inconsistent performance were due instead to her core phonological processing problems, which affected her ability to remember verbal sequences (such as complex multiple directions), memorize lists, and even to read. Her spelling tests varied so much because of the amount of practice time she and her mother spent at home, though clearly, her spontaneous spelling was consistently poor. Brianne's behavior problems—moodiness being most prominent—reflected her increasing recognition of her problems and helplessness. The fact that she tended to be very quiet and reserved may also have reflected her problem in finding words to express herself.

COMMUNICATION

Other children struggle not only with reading but in multiple areas of communication. Oral language problems can exist in syntax (the way words are put together to form phrases), semantics (the meanings of words), morphology (word formation), phonology (speech sounds), articulation (producing sounds), and pragmatics (the relationship between words and their users) (Gibbs & Cooper, 1989). Communication involves both receptive and expressive language skills. In essence, "receptive language" refers to receiving communication, whereas "expressive language" refers to producing language. Children with receptive language disorders may have problems comprehending single words or may struggle to understand when words are strung together in sentences. They may understand only a part of what is said and respond to that part, or may be entirely confused by what they perceive to be a jumble of words. In a sense, children with significant receptive language problems experience the world in ways similar to someone in a foreign country. Although the sounds of the foreign language can be heard and perhaps even reproduced, the conversations seem meaningless. Children with receptive language problems often also have some difficulties with expressive language.

In contrast, children with expressive language problems can understand what is said to them but may communicate with gestures and in other nonverbal ways, because they have difficulty producing intelligible speech. This is different from speech disorders, such as stuttering and articulation problems, that also interfere with learning but are generally not considered to be a type of learning disability. Rather, expressive language problems can be so significant that a child's speech is meaningless. Usually, expressive language problems are less obvious. For example, 9-year-old Gwen seemed to have a limited vocabulary because she constantly used the word *thing,* and because she tended to describe an object rather than name it (e.g., "that thing you write with" instead of "pencil"). In actuality, she probably had dysnomia, or a deficit in recalling specific words (Lerner, 1993). This deficit was responsible for another student spending over an hour to write five sentences.

Severe receptive or expressive language problems rarely go unnoticed, and generally, such children are referred for a psychoeducational evaluation early on. Often, a child may be overly quiet, for example, or may be described by parents as slow to speak. It is certainly possible, however, for children with milder difficulties to be undiagnosed and to have their problems attributed to other reasons, such as being "shy" or "in their own world." It is also highly possible that the deficits are in both receptive and expressive areas, resulting in a more diffuse presentation that is harder to identify.

WRITING

Children can have difficulty in many written-language skills, which include handwriting, spelling, punctuation, capitalization, and composition (O'Shea et al., 1998). Perhaps the most common disorder of written expression is a deficiency in spelling. Spelling problems may be a sign of dyslexia and may reflect an underlying problem with phonological processing. Specifically, if a child cannot identify the sound units that make up a word, she or he probably will not be able to accurately combine letters to form the word. However, spelling problems may also be separate from dyslexia and indicate problems in areas other than phonological processing. For example, a child may have difficulty visualizing a word or may struggle when retrieving the word from memory without other contextual or visual cues (Lerner, 1993).

The other common writing disorder is in handwriting. A child with almost illegible handwriting should not be dismissed as "messy" or "careless," but should be evaluated for an underlying learning disability. Handwriting difficulties are considered to be a deficit in written expression and may also be part of a larger nonverbal learning disability. Very poor handwriting may be due to visual-motor deficits, problems with visual perception, fine-motor coordination problems, and/or compromised spatial abilities. The term *dysgraphia* is typically reserved for severe handwriting problems. Although proper penmanship might seem archaic, dysgraphia and even more minor handwriting disorders have significant repercussions in later learning. For example, because of his terrible handwriting, 10-year-old Michael tended to avoid all language arts assignments, even electing not to do tasks he could easily accomplish because it was too tiring to try to write legibly. Children who are unable to write letters of the same size and to maintain an even line will likely have trouble doing math problems that require accurate placement of digits in columns (e.g., borrowing).

ARITHMETIC

Problems with mathematics may stem from a variety of deficits. Careful assessment must determine if the deficiencies truly reside in mathematics, or if they are more reflective of problems of spatial arrangement, attention and concentration, or even reading comprehension. For example, a student who is consistently unable to do word problems may have intact calculation skills but may not be able to read well enough to comprehend the mathematical operation being required. True math disabilities involve problems with math concepts and skills, including computation, problem solving, geometry, mental calculations, estimation, probability, statistics, decimals, measurement, and fractions (O'Shea et al., 1998).

Some use the term *dyscalculia* to refer to a primary disability in learning computation and math concepts (Fleischner & Manheimer, 1997). These skill areas include one-to-one correspondence, part-to-whole relationships (e.g., fractions), place value, as well as basic skills such as subtraction and multiplication. Problems with core math skills may be hard to detect, because students with dyscalculia may try to get around their difficulties by relying on counting for computing basic facts, rather than on recall (Fleischner, Garnett, & Shepherd, 1982), which can hinder math achievement significantly. Because of their difficulties comprehending the concepts behind the operations, children with dyscalculia may struggle to learn math despite frequent drills and instruction.

Fleischner and Manheimer (1997) recommend using a five-step sequence when introducing math concepts to make them more understandable to your students, particularly those with learning disabilities. The sequence begins with concrete representation (e.g., use of manipulative materials), even if such concreteness is atypical for the age of your students. Next, use pictorial representation, such as by asking your students to demonstrate their understanding with pictures or other figures. Follow this with deliberate linking of the concrete and pictorial representations by having students discuss and explain their reasoning. Fourth, make sure that your students understand the symbols being used. Last, "abstract," or check to see if your students can state the steps to solving a problem in a way that makes sense to other students.

Math disabilities may appear as a circumscribed problem area or may be part of a broader neurologically based condition. For example, developmental

Gerstmann syndrome, which includes a constellation of dysgraphia, dyscalculia, and neurological soft-signs (subtle physical abnormalities), is considered a nonverbal learning disorder (Benson & Geschwind, 1970).

NONVERBAL LEARNING DISABILITIES

Identification of a nonverbal learning disability may be more difficult than a language-based disability, because it is less well understood. Characteristics of a nonverbal learning disability include tactile-perceptual deficits; psychomotor coordination problems; visual, spatial, and organizational difficulties; problems adapting to novel and complex situations; poor mathematics abilities; and problems in social perception and judgment (Rourke, Young, & Leenars, 1989). Signs of a Nonverbal Learning Disability, found at the end of this chapter, may help you identify this learning disability in your students. In addition, the following case study is an example of how a nonverbal learning disability may appear in your classroom.

✦ CASE STUDY: The Child With a Nonverbal Learning Disability

Billy was obviously smart. He could easily outwit his peers with his biting sarcasm and annoyed his teachers with his relentless probing questions. He regularly infuriated his fifth-grade teacher by finding shortcuts. If he could still get a decent grade by doing only half of an assignment, he would. What made it so frustrating was that Billy seemed to perform below his superior intellect, despite his parents' and teachers' efforts. His work seemed carelessly done, and it was barely legible on most days. The situation was worst in math, in which Billy simply refused to do work, claiming that it was unnecessary for his future career as a lawyer. In addition, Billy and his parents were locked into a daily struggle to get him to do homework, with Billy typically winning. Socially, Billy didn't seem to fit in with his peers. During recess, he was often alone while the others played Nerf football. He seemed to alienate himself by using vocabulary above the level of his peers. Sometimes, it seemed Billy was not even fully aware of how much his words could hurt others.

Billy's learning difficulties were difficult to discern because of his clear verbal strengths. He had an exceptional verbal memory, such as memorizing parts of stories, as well as solid reading and language skills. Attributing his performance to lack of motivation would not be far-fetched, since Billy stated his dislike of math outright. However, Billy's pattern of underachievement also suggests a possible nonverbal learning disability. He had always struggled with basic math concepts but found creative ways to compensate. For example, rather than read the clock incorrectly, Billy wore a digital watch. For a long time, he secretly used a calculator to do math problems. He had to talk himself through computations, almost having to make them into sentences before he could answer them (e.g., the problem $100 \times \frac{1}{4} = ?$ became "¼ of 100 is 100 divided into 4 parts, which is . . .").

(continued)

Billy's disastrous written work was not due to carelessness. His handwriting was atrocious, even if he painstakingly wrote out his assignments. His word spacing was inconsistent; letter sizes varied greatly; and he used an odd mix of capital and lowercase letters in the same word. He lacked fine motor coordination in general, as well as hand-eye coordination, making it difficult for him to engage in sports. His defensiveness about his coordination problems frequently triggered his mean verbal lashings.

Billy's social difficulties were also affected by his impaired spatial abilities. He often stood too close to people, which made his peers uncomfortable. His social problems were also due to his impaired social cognition, since he had trouble discerning others' emotions from their facial expressions or tone of voice. He relied on his verbal skills to deal with social discomfort but nevertheless seemed to have difficulty when encountering new situations.

OTHER LEARNING PROBLEMS

Other deficits can also affect achievement and are increasingly considered to be learning disabilities. Although these are not formally recognized by schools as necessitating special services, it is helpful to be aware of the growing support for identification of disorders in executive functioning, memory, and self-regulation.

The term *executive functioning* refers to higher-order processes such as planning ahead and organizing information. These functions affect a variety of experiences, making it difficult to pinpoint a learning disability. An example of higher-order problems is difficulty in concept formation. As a result, the child may not be able to generalize from one learning situation to another (Abrams, 1986). It is as if the child has to relearn the concept for every assignment or application. For instance, Stephanie's fourth-grade teacher constantly complained that she seemed to understand what she was teaching one day, then forgot it the next.

Other executive functions include selective attention (e.g., being able to screen out stimuli and focus only on something specific) and inhibitory control (e.g., holding back one's urges). ADHD is considered by most educators as more of a behavioral disorder than a learning disorder (and consequently is discussed more fully in Chapter 2). However, new research suggests that children with ADHD have fundamental deficits in regulating their internal arousal and attention, as well as impulse control and activity level (Shelton & Barkley, 1995). These deficits in executive functioning imply that ADHD is related to the fundamental processes of learning, not just to behavior (Pennington, 1991). Interestingly, approximately one fourth of all children with ADHD will also have at least one type of additional learning disability in math, reading, or spelling (Barkley, 1990), further suggesting a need for reconceptualization.

Memory is complex. Remembering something requires noticing it, focusing on it, registering it, storing the information in some meaningful way, and recalling it. Problems with any of these skills result in great difficulties acquiring new information and retrieving previously learned information. Children with fundamental deficits in memory often experience a vicious cycle of learning problems that exists across subject matter. For example, sixth-grader Jin struggled in almost all academic subjects, leading her teachers to believe she was simply a below-average student. However, her worst subject was clearly social studies, because she had a terrible time memorizing all the names, dates, and places. Children with memory deficits may also be seen as having problems in attention or concentration, when in actuality the deficits are more serious.

The concept of self-regulation is fairly new and refers to the ability to monitor one's internal processes and adjust them accordingly to meet situational demands. For example, after seeing a frightening movie, you use various ways to calm yourself down so you can have a pleasant conversation with your friend, rather than feel hypervigilant and suspicious of everything around you in the restaurant. Children with disorders of self-regulation may have difficulty being aware of their heightened arousal and may not be able to shift their internal activity level to adjust to a new situation. For example, a child with poor self-regulatory abilities may not be able to make the transition from gym class to silent reading without significant external prompting and structure (e.g., constant reminders to "calm down"). Problems in self-regulation are especially relevant in emotional disorders and will be discussed in more detail in Chapter 2. Cognitive self-regulation, such as being able to set goals, monitor one's progress, and adjust effort accordingly, is also a necessary part of learning (Bronson, 2000). Not being able to "talk oneself through" a difficult task makes problem solving more difficult and learning more arduous.

There is also growing recognition that social, emotional, and behavioral problems typically considered to be childhood psychological or emotional disorders have a strong impact on school achievement and learning. These conditions are discussed separately in Chapter 2 to distinguish them from disabilities based primarily in the learning processes identified here. The following case study, shared by third-grade teacher Sarah Ascheman, provides a common example of how multiple deficits can affect a child's learning.

❖ CASE STUDY: **The Child With Multiple Learning Disabilities**

Edgar came into my third-grade classroom at 8.5 years old and reading and writing at a low first-grade level. He had a sight word vocabulary of 35 words and minimal phonemic awareness. Edgar's oral language skills were limited as well. Edgar is a second-language learner . . . having difficulty recalling many English words and often having trouble finding the words he wanted in Spanish as well. Edgar would come over to speak to me, begin his sentence, pause, and then say he had forgotten what he wanted to say.

Edgar has a very short attention span. He is usually up out of his seat within a minute of sitting down and walking around the classroom. When the class is listening to a story on the rug, Edgar is either walking around, playing with something, or disturbing other children. When reading with Edgar one-on-one, he pauses several times to talk about other things.

(continued)

❖ CASE STUDY: Continued

Edgar also has a great deal of difficulty interacting with other children. Edgar will talk with other students, pick fights, or steal from other students when they are trying to work. The other students also become easily frustrated with him in a cooperative working environment because of his struggle with staying on task. The other students often tease him about his inability to read. . . .

In the beginning of the year, [classroom] modifications were made to move him academically and meet his attentional needs. Edgar worked one-on-one with teachers, tutors, a literacy coach, classroom assistants, and was peer tutored several times a day. He received intensive phonemic awareness and sight word recognition teaching on a daily basis. He attended literacy intervention classes for 1 hour 2 days a week after school with me for a majority of the year. All tasks that he was given were in no more than 15-minute blocks of time, and directions given were simple and concise. All of these modifications helped some, but his academic growth was not at full grade level. . . .

After assessing Edgar, I made a referral within the first few weeks of school. . . . Edgar's mother made a request for testing in April, and his testing began shortly after. At his IEP meeting, the tests from the school psychologist and resource teacher showed that he had average cognitive ability for his age but had visual, auditory, and verbal learning disabilities. The psychologist also suggested that he be tested further for ADHD.

REMEDIATING LEARNING DISABILITIES

If your student has been identified as having a learning disability, special remedial services, such as daily resource room time, will be included in his or her individualized education program (IEP). In some schools, many of the learning objectives written into the IEP are considered to be the primary responsibility of the special education or resource room teacher. The trend toward inclusion, however, means that more often, these learning objectives will be the shared responsibility of the general education teacher and learning specialists. Most schools have established Child Study/Resource Teams, which typically consist of the principal, special educators, resource specialists, regular education classroom teachers, and referring teachers (Hayek, 1987). These are forums for teachers to problem-solve and develop classroom intervention strategies prior to formal referral for special education services. This type of collaborative approach to helping children with disabilities is one in which all members of a problem-solving team participate as equals.

In addition to the interventions agreed upon by your multidisciplinary team, you can implement the numerous classroom interventions and accommodations discussed throughout this book. Ideas for reading, writing, and arithmetic interventions and accommodations can be found at the end of this chapter.

SUMMARY

The term *learning disability* refers to a discrepancy between intellectual ability and achievement in one or more areas of reading, writing, and mathematics. The most well-understood learning disability is dyslexia, which involves difficulty in processing the sound units that make up language and is characterized by poor reading skills. Other learning disabilities include problems with receptive and/or expressive language, dysgraphia (disorder of handwriting) and dyscalculia (mathematics disorder). Nonverbal learning disorders are more difficult to identify because they include difficulties that vary from social troubles to spatial problems. As research grows, other types of learning disabilities (e.g., in memory, attention, and self-regulation) are being considered as explanations for children's problems with learning and relationships.

SIGNS OF A READING DISORDER

BASIC SKILLS:

- ❑ Has problems learning color or letter names
- ❑ Does not have solid grasp of letter-sound correspondences
- ❑ Does poorly on phonics assignments
- ❑ Has problems remembering basic math facts

READING:

- ❑ Lacks age-appropriate number of sight words
- ❑ Oral reading lacks fluency or is halting
- ❑ Has persistent decoding difficulties
- ❑ Doesn't understand what he/she just read aloud
- ❑ Reading comprehension is derailed by decoding problems
- ❑ Transposes words
- ❑ Reading abilities inconsistent with apparent intelligence and vocabulary
- ❑ Interchanges articles and prepositions (e.g., "a" and "the")
- ❑ Frequent substitution of words that are visually similar (e.g., *want* for *what*)
- ❑ Slow rate of reading
- ❑ Words are fragmented when read
- ❑ Adds words while reading
- ❑ Continues to rely on finger pointing (for older students)
- ❑ Continues to move lips while reading (for older students)

WRITING:

- ❏ Makes repeated letter reversals (after 9 years of age)
- ❏ Makes spelling errors on sight words
- ❏ Spelling errors frequently include omission of consonants
- ❏ Missequences syllables (e.g., *aminals* for *animals*)
- ❏ Writes slowly or laboriously
- ❏ Makes number reversals

SPOKEN LANGUAGE:

- ❏ Has difficulties finding the right word
- ❏ Has trouble remembering verbal sequences (e.g., phone numbers, directions, months of the year)
- ❏ Seems to mishear words (e.g., *bat* instead of *pat*)
- ❏ Has a limited vocabulary

BEHAVIOR:

- ❏ Dislikes reading or avoids it
- ❏ Has behavior problems during or before reading time or activities with significant reading
- ❏ Refuses to do homework requiring reading
- ❏ Is disruptive during class silent reading times
- ❏ Seems to look only at pictures in storybooks and ignores text
- ❏ Has problems during class library time (e.g., avoids choosing a book)

SIGNS OF A NONVERBAL LEARNING DISABILITY

SPATIAL

- ❑ Has trouble remembering how to get places
- ❑ Frequently gets lost
- ❑ Confuses left and right
- ❑ Has trouble telling time
- ❑ Has poor hand-eye coordination
- ❑ Has trouble completing puzzles
- ❑ Doesn't draw well
- ❑ Desk/book bag is very disorganized
- ❑ Has poor sense of interpersonal space

SOCIAL

- ❑ Has trouble figuring out others' emotional states
- ❑ Doesn't seem aware of social nuances
- ❑ Appears oblivious of the social impact of his/her actions
- ❑ Increasing social withdrawal (for older children)
- ❑ Has problems adapting to new situations
- ❑ Does not read nonverbal behavior cues effectively

MATH

- ❑ Struggles with basic math concepts
- ❑ Has trouble keeping math columns aligned
- ❑ Becomes confused on multistep calculations
- ❑ Math answers are wildly incorrect

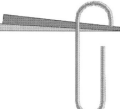

WRITING

- ❏ Has poor handwriting, especially under time pressure
- ❏ Writing on unlined paper is difficult and disorganized
- ❏ Misspells age-appropriate words
- ❏ Has poor fine-motor control
- ❏ Has problems copying from the blackboard
- ❏ Writes very slowly
- ❏ Has awkward pencil grip
- ❏ Letters appear jagged and inconsistent
- ❏ Has trouble keeping a left margin (margin drifts significantly)

BEHAVIOR

- ❏ Dislikes or avoids math
- ❏ Dislikes or avoids art
- ❏ Refuses to do written work or homework
- ❏ Seems isolated from peers
- ❏ Does not engage in sports

INTERVENTIONS AND ACCOMMODATIONS FOR LEARNING DISABILITIES

Reading

- Extensive phonics drills, ideally done in context
- Extensive letter-sound correspondence drills, ideally done in context
- Sight word recognition drills, ideally done in context
- Use of visual images corresponding to letter sounds (e.g., "i" becomes the feather in an Indian headdress)
- Textbooks, and so forth, are read aloud to the student (or use of tape-recorded textbooks)
- Extra time for tests (so content, not reading speed, is assessed)
- Interactive computer reading programs (e.g., CD-ROMS)

Writing

- Use of a computer or word processor for written assignments and note taking
- Permission to write in print rather than cursive
- Use of a template to maintain margins (e.g., a "window frame")
- Acceptance of homework dictated by student and written by parents
- Use of electronic or computer spell checkers
- Permission to do oral testing (so content, not writing ability, is assessed)
- Multisensory approach to learning spelling (e.g., tracing the word and saying it)

Arithmetic

- Use of graph paper for calculations
- Use of manipulative materials (e.g., base 10 blocks), even in upper grades
- Use of calculator
- Placement of a number line on the student's desk for addition and subtraction
- Use of basic math fact charts to refer to when solving problems
- Use of color-coding steps in multistep problems
- Use of a deck of cards or real money to learn number concepts

2

COMMON SOCIAL, EMOTIONAL, AND BEHAVIORAL DISORDERS

*One time a parent threatened to kill me. The family was very abusive,
but I couldn't let the child be abusive to classmates. Children that
witness many horrific things bring the baggage to school, and
[I want to] get them to . . . feel safe [in] one place, our classroom.*

—Donna-Jean F. Wosencroft
Fifth-grade teacher
29 years of teaching experience
Providence, Rhode Island

All teachers have students who are anxious, seem withdrawn, or act out in class. These emotions and behaviors should be expected as being within the realm of everyday life. However, for some children, these difficulties are extreme enough to impair their daily functioning. Formal classification of an emotional disturbance means that the child's "persistent and consistent severe behavior disabilities . . . disrupt the student's or others' learning processes [and that their] inability to achieve academic progress or satisfactory interpersonal relationships cannot be attributed to physical, sensory or intellectual impairments" (O'Shea, O'Shea, & Algozzine, 1998, pp. 21-22). Teachers and parents may be reluctant to refer a child for social, emotional, and behavioral problems for fear of the repercussions of labeling a child as having "Emotional Disturbance (ED)." However, it is important to recognize when these problems are beyond the norm and when intervention is essential. This chapter discusses social, emotional, and behavioral disorders likely to be encountered in the classroom.

One way of thinking about various social, emotional, and behavioral disorders is to consider the outward manifestation of the child's inner state. The category of "internalizing" behaviors includes social withdrawal, depression, loneliness, and anxiety, all reflecting turmoil that is kept inside. In contrast, "externalizing" behavior—such as aggression, disruptive behavior, and oppositionality—is directing one's turmoil outward. People may display all these behaviors. However, each person has a natural tendency or preference toward internalizing or externalizing, likely due to genetic factors (Gjone & Stevenson, 1997). Children who are depressed may also experience significant anxiety, for example, but may not strike out at their peers or defy the teacher. Other children may seem to "have a chip on their shoulders" and be easily angered and verbally hostile when upset, rather than withdrawing.

Both types of behavior have significant repercussions for learning and achievement. However, attention is more likely to be given to externalizing behavior disorders, because they tend to be disruptive to others. Students with internalizing behavior disorders are generally underreferred for special services, because they do not present classroom management difficulties for teachers (Kauffman, 1993). Furthermore, Gresham, Lane, MacMillan, and Bocian (1999) found that at-risk students with internalizing problems have many negative comments in their cumulative files (e.g., "is immature" and "is lazy and stubborn"), suggesting that their social and emotional difficulties were noticed but not necessarily identified as needing referral for special intervention.

Signs of an Emotional Disorder, found at the end of this chapter, points out common characteristics of children who are depressed, anxious, or have a behavioral disorder. This checklist is not meant to enable you to diagnose a specific psychiatric disorder but to increase your awareness of when such problems may warrant mental health services. If your students display several characteristics in one or more areas, they may be experiencing significant emotional disturbance that requires a referral to support personnel, such as your school psychologist, for the appropriate services.

DEPRESSION

Over the past two decades, childhood depression has received increasing attention. It is estimated that 0.4 to 2.5% of children are clinically depressed

(McCauley, Myers, Mitchell, Calderon, Schloredt, & Treder, 1993) and that the average duration of a major depressive disorder in children and adolescents is 7 to 9 months (Birmaher et al., 1996). This is significant, because a child may not recover from a major depressive disorder for an entire school year, which interferes with critical learning and development. When you think of depression in youth, you might imagine a sullen, withdrawn teenager. However, this may or may not depict the younger child who is depressed. Elementary-aged children with depression may appear irritable, apathetic, distracted, and be accident prone in addition to feeling sad. Depressed preschoolers may also appear hyperactive and aggressive or oppositional, in part because they do not have adequate language to communicate their feelings. More commonly, depressed children experience episodes of sadness intermixed with acting out and academic underachievement (Aylward, 1985; Reynolds, 1990). Unlike adults and older adolescents, in whom depression is far more prevalent in females (American Psychiatric Association, 1994), childhood depression is found equally in boys and girls (Wright-Strawderman & Watson, 1992).

The reasons for a child's depression may be easily identifiable, such as when a student's parents are undergoing a divorce, or may be much less obvious and difficult to discern. Some children may be chronically depressed rather than reacting to a specific stressor, and this depression can last for years (Cicchetti & Toth, 1998). For example, ever since his father left the family 2 years ago, 9-year-old Ryan had been listless, withdrawn, and had little interest in doing much of anything. He also became encopretic (having problems controlling his bowels), but his extreme reluctance to talk about his encopresis made it almost impossible to help him. Depression often coexists with other psychological disorders, most often anxiety disorders (Kovacs, 1996). In addition, depression can have a great impact on a child's academic and social functioning. Childhood depression must be taken seriously. Even young children can become so overwhelmed that they contemplate suicide, and they can choose methods of self-harm that are lethal (e.g., running into traffic).

ANXIETY

As with depression, children experiencing significant anxiety may be easily identified because of their demeanor (e.g., seeming nervous or hypervigilant), or their anxiety may be less obvious. Often, children who are anxious complain of physical discomfort, such as headaches, stomachaches, or fatigue. It is helpful to question students about their symptoms, and ruling out any medically based problems is important. The anxiety experienced may be related to something at school (e.g., teasing by peers at lunch or recess), may be more generalized (e.g., the child who worries about everything), or may stem from specific issues such as learning problems or separation anxiety.

Separation anxiety disorder is a common anxiety disorder among elementary school-aged children. These children fear separation from the significant adults in their lives, often because of insecurity or fear that harm may befall their caretakers. Children with separation anxiety may seem particularly clingy and in need of attention. Others may refuse to go to school or, once at school, may protest excessively when leaving their parent or guardian (e.g., tantrums, hysterical crying). These children also may have frequent physical complaints. These complaints of discomfort may be motivated by a desire to reunite with their caregivers (e.g., parents are called to take their sick child home). Alternatively, their anxiety could be affecting their physical health (e.g., excess acid in the stomach leading to frequent stomachaches). Separation anxiety occurs in both younger and older children, as with sixth-grader Craig, who suddenly began refusing school because of his fears and eventually had to repeat the grade because of all the time he had missed.

Anxiety disorders are closely related to other emotional disturbances, particularly depression and low self-esteem (Rawson, 1992). In fact, there is some indication that they may precede depressive disorders (Kovacs, 1996). Anxiety can also create a vicious cycle. Children who are highly anxious may interpret ambiguous situations in a threatening manner, resulting in further anxiety (Barrett, Rapee, Dadds, & Ryan, 1996). In addition, avoidance of the feared situation perpetuates the initial anxiety by reinforcing the idea that the child cannot handle the situation. For example, 8-year-old Brandy shied away from anything involving numbers because of her significant math disability. This meant that she even avoided doing simple things like helping put together next month's calendar and passing out supplies (because it might involve counting). Brandy's extreme avoidance significantly interfered with her ability to develop her math skills.

LOW SELF-ESTEEM AND POOR SELF-CONCEPT

Every teacher can think of a student who has low self-esteem. Whether this is a child who is not able to accept a compliment, does not put much effort into schoolwork, or generally seems to dislike himself or herself, problems with self-esteem are common. There is no consensus on what constitutes self-esteem. Some make a distinction that self-esteem is primarily based in emotions (e.g., "I feel fat"), whereas self-concept is based more on thoughts (e.g., "I am unlovable") (Haney & Durlak, 1998). Regardless, the importance of adequate self-esteem and positive self-concept has been widely recognized in intervention efforts. Intervention in these areas can yield positive changes in other areas of adjustment, such as academic performance and problematic behavior (Haney & Durlak, 1998).

Self-esteem is not just a global concept; it includes aspects such as our view of ourselves, awareness and acknowledgment of talents, methods of dealing with our failings, and the ability to cope with how others view us. Problems can occur in a specific aspect of self-esteem. For example, a child may feel confident socially but not in academic settings (e.g., the class clown), resulting in poor academic self-concept but adequate interpersonal self-concept.

Alternatively, a pervasive negative sense of self or an overall feeling of being flawed may affect all areas of a child's functioning. Significantly low self-esteem and poor self-concept prevent children from objectively evaluating their skills and talents, because their negative self-view becomes the lens through which all information is filtered. Low self-esteem can also be a major component of a vicious cycle of poor performance. Children who feel they are "stupid" may not exert themselves on a math assignment, for example. The poor grade they receive confirms their original view and lowers their self-concept and motivation even further. They may have little motivation to take risks as well, which also limits their abilities and experiences. Low self-esteem can also appear as a fear of failure, avoiding everything that might remind children of their feelings of worthlessness.

It is easy to see how low self-esteem could contribute to anxiety, depression, behavioral problems, and poor school performance. The following case study provides an example of how these issues can interact in a student. For intervention to be most effective, efforts should target improving self-esteem and self-concept directly, rather than "hoping that SE/SC can be modified indirectly by working on other areas of adjustment" (Hanley & Durlak, 1998, p. 429). Comprehensive self-esteem programs abound, but there are also specific activities that a teacher can easily incorporate into the school day. Classroom interventions to boost children's self-esteem can be found in Chapters 3, 6, and 7. The overall goal of such interventions should be to build the child's sense of self without reinforcing a self-centeredness that negates others.

❖ CASE STUDY: **The Anxious and Insecure Child**

Ever since he was a toddler, Evan seemed to be a perfectionist. He disliked getting dirty, and consequently, he avoided playing in the sandbox at daycare. He frequently displayed frustration when things couldn't be done right, such as not being able to cut a perfect circle during art or refusing to do work if his pencil wasn't sharpened properly. Evan also seemed to become unglued when change occurred, and it took him quite a while to adjust to new things in his daily routine. In the lower grades, tantrums were frequent but could be avoided fairly easily with some planning and accommodation for his eccentricities.

By fourth grade, however, Evan's increasing anxiety was becoming troubling. He began to anticipate failure or difficulty and, as a result, would avoid tasks without even attempting them. For example, if no lined paper was available for writing, Evan would procrastinate beginning the assignment, eventually failing to do it altogether. He avoided taking risks, such as volunteering answers aloud, and didn't like to try tasks that might be a bit challenging.

When Evan did do his assignments, he often spent hours laboring over them. One time, a history report was turned in by his mother a week late. Apparently, Evan wasn't pleased with the results of his cover drawing of soldiers, which he had painstakingly traced from the encyclopedia, and had decided not to turn it in. He also had difficulty accepting his mistakes. Rather than redo assignments for make-up credit, he typically threw such indications of his imperfection away. He was so sensitive to criticism that he would completely shut down—refusing to speak or respond—if he felt he was being corrected in any way. At the same time, Evan tended to blame himself for many failures that were not entirely of his own doing. As a result, he spent much of the day alternating between worrying and brooding. Although he had the cognitive ability to do well in school, his emotional problems interfered with his achievement. Evan's grades began to slip considerably, prompting a referral for special education services.

AGGRESSION

Aggression in children is a serious problem, reflected all too often in media accounts of school shootings, children killing other children, and early adolescents being tried as adults for heinous crimes. Unfortunately, the incidents are not isolated. Rather, there seems to be an overall increase in disobedience and aggression in children (Coie & Dodge, 1998). Aggression can range from bullying and oppositionality to destructive acting out. It may be directed at specific individuals who share common characteristics, may be focused on objects rather than people, or may appear indiscriminate. The roots of childhood aggression are varied. Children may act out if they are unable to otherwise express frustration. Anger in response to life stressors may be released physically. For example, second-grader Kenny announced his parents' divorce by throwing his school desk against the wall. Children may also have learned that they get what they want when they bully others. Some children who are victimized cope by taking on the role of the aggressor so that they do not feel so vulnerable. Poor social skills can also result in aggressive behavior. Regardless of its origins, aggression in early childhood is a strong warning that significant problems are present that require immediate attention. Helping aggressive children to manage their anger and destructive urges is imperative. The energy that is contained in a child's anger must be rechanneled into more productive activities.

Early aggression also has implications for the child's future. Research suggests that early anger reactions in children as young as 4- to 6-year-olds are predictive of social functioning years later (Eisenberg et al., 1999). For example, 4- to 6-year-old children who engaged in physical retaliation and other aggression were less socially appropriate and reported to have more problem behaviors 4 years later. Early acting-out behavior, such as temper tantrums and troublesomeness, has also been linked to adolescent and adult antisocial behavior (Patterson, DeBaryshe, & Ramsey, 1989). Highly aggressive children also appear to be at risk for significant disturbance in adulthood, including criminal behavior, alcohol and drug abuse, and mental illness (Farrington, 1995). Of course, not all aggressive children will become violent adults. In addition, there may be substantial discontinuity in aggressive behavior over time (e.g., a child may actually stop displaying aggressive behavior for a period of time) (Loeber & Stouthamer-Loeber, 1998). Even so, early aggressive behavior can have a lasting impact on a child's social and academic outcomes and should not be ignored.

ATTENTION-DEFICIT/
HYPERACTIVITY DISORDER

Although you may encounter aggressive children, more likely you will have more students who are disruptive and inattentive. Disruptive behavior is not necessarily aggressive and may reflect poor social skills or problems with self-regulation. It is perhaps the greatest source of stress for teachers (Borg, Riding, & Falzon, 1991). One of the most common disruptive behavior disorders is Attention-Deficit/Hyperactivity Disorder (ADHD), which is estimated to occur in 3 to 5% of school-aged children (American Psychiatric Association, 1994). You may be surprised at these low numbers, given the volumes of research on ADHD and by how much attention it is given by the popular press. Indeed, more than one teacher has been heard to remark that "it seems like half of my class has ADHD." Some believe that the term is overused, or even misused, for problems related more to "poor parenting" than attention. Others argue that ADHD is present not only in children but in adults as well (Resnick, 2000), perhaps due to neurologically based underlying deficits.

As currently defined by the *Diagnostic and Statistical Manual of Mental Disorders* (4th ed.), ADHD reflects a "persistent pattern of inattention and/or hyperactivity-impulsivity that is more frequent and severe than is typically observed in individuals at a comparable level of development" (American Psychiatric Association, 1994). For this diagnosis to be accurately applied, the behavioral disturbance must exceed the wide spectrum of age-appropriate expectations, must be demonstrated in more than one setting (e.g., both at home and school), and must not be better explained by another condition, such as an emotional disorder.

There are two distinct subtypes of ADHD: Predominantly Inattentive and Predominantly Hyperactive-Impulsive Type (American Psychiatric Association, 1994). Children may also demonstrate symptoms of both, reflected in a Combined Type. Often, children with hyperactivity and impulsivity are more readily identified than children who are inattentive because of their disruptiveness in the classroom (e.g., failing to stay seated, not being able to wait one's turn, blurting out answers). Both types of children, as well as children with ADHD Combined Type, have fundamental deficits in regulating their internal arousal and attention, as well as their impulse control and activity level (Shelton & Barkley, 1995). What this means is that once revved up, they may not be able to calm down, or when tired, they may not be able to muster up energy to work undistracted. These difficulties are not just behavior problems; they also affect learning, since focused attention and intense concentration are needed to acquire new concepts. The following case study illustrates how ADHD Inattentive Type can affect a child's social relationships and achievement.

✧ CASE STUDY: **The Child With ADHD Inattentive Type**

In comparison with her fifth-grade peers, Nancy seemed immature. She was shorter than the other children and seemed less socially adept than her classmates. Although she hadn't caused any real trouble in the past, the discrepancy between Nancy and her peers was becoming increasingly of concern. The fifth-grade teachers expected some degree of independence and initiative taking from their students. They repeatedly expressed frustration with Nancy's childishness, forgetfulness, and constant need for direction.

Nancy's desk and book bag were always a disaster. She often couldn't find things, including her books and school supplies. Half-completed assignments

(continued)

were stuffed everywhere. When confronted about her disorganization, Nancy simply laughed in a silly manner and said, "That's nothing! You should see my room at home!" Nancy's peers were also beginning to ostracize her. She couldn't seem to remember task directions for group assignments and frequently lost track of what the class was studying, such as needing to be told where to start for round robin reading or what question to answer when it was her turn. She sometimes seemed to be in her own world, appearing somewhat surprised when called upon.

Nancy displayed classic symptoms of ADHD Inattentive Type. Her core difficulty was in sustaining attention and concentration. In the early grades, Nancy's problems had not drawn much attention, because they were shared by many of her peers. However, as classroom demands for greater independence increased, her deficits became more noticeable. Attributing her disability to childishness was not helpful. It merely increased her teacher's frustration and caused Nancy to revert to joking and silliness as coping methods. Correctly identifying her deficits eventually led to coordinated efforts to teach Nancy strategies for organization, planning ahead, and regulating attention.

OTHER DISRUPTIVE BEHAVIOR

Other disruptive behavior disorders include oppositional defiant disorder, characterized by a pattern of resistance toward authority, and conduct disorder, which reflects pervasive disregard for social norms and rules. These disorders are thought to have a primarily emotional and psychological basis, rather than a root in neurological deficits. Children who meet criteria for these disorders are usually quickly identified by their teachers, because their behavioral disturbance exceeds the norm. Because of the nature of the disorders, these children require substantial therapeutic intervention that is beyond the scope of the regular classroom.

Some disruptive behavior is the result of social skills deficits. Currently, there is no formally accepted definition of social skills disorder, but social skills problems can be significant enough to warrant attention and intervention. Some children have problems identifying or interpreting social cues. For example, they may not notice that their peers are becoming annoyed. As a result, they may not be able to generate an appropriate social response (e.g., stopping their annoying behavior), often resulting in their rejection. Repeated experiences like this reinforce the child's isolation, further exacerbating the original social skills deficits. A child with significant social skills deficits may be a social outcast or someone who just "doesn't seem to fit in." Other social skills problems include having difficulty taking the perspective of another, not being aware of situational social demands, and lacking basic interpersonal skills. Nine-year-old Kirstie, for example, seemed self-centered and was oblivious to others' wishes. She genuinely seemed surprised when reminded that others had different opinions and did not necessarily see things her way. Not surprisingly, Kirstie didn't have any close friends and was generally viewed as a nuisance by adults.

TREATMENT

It would be unreasonable to assume that the classroom teacher should be primarily responsible for treating social, emotional, and behavioral disorders. Forgoing a math lesson and ignoring 30 other students to attend to 1 child may be necessary on occasion, but it is hardly good practice over the long run. These disorders require specific treatment that is typically provided by mental health professionals. It is the teacher's job to minimize the effects of these disorders on a student's learning and classroom experience.

For children who have social, emotional, and behavioral problems that are not serious enough to be classified as emotional disturbance, being understanding and perhaps providing a little extra attention is helpful. Providing a shoulder to cry on or a listening ear for your students does wonders. Sometimes it is all they need to be able to move on from an engulfing emotional state. In addition, such support is good for the classroom community, not only because it creates a healthy learning environment but also because a little proactive support can reduce the need for later crisis management. More extensive discussion of classroom strategies to deal with the impact of these disorders can be found in Part II.

SUMMARY

Social, emotional, and behavioral disorders can be conceptualized as being focused within the child (internalizing) or directed toward others (externalizing). When a child's turmoil is kept within, depression, anxiety, and low self-esteem may follow. Externalizing disorders, such as aggression, ADHD, and disruptive behavior, are more visible because of the classroom management consequences. Both require referral for intervention and support, because they prevent a child from engaging in normal age-appropriate activities and can significantly interfere with learning and relationships. Primary treatment should be provided by mental health professionals, but you can use interventions found in Part II to supplement these efforts.

SIGNS OF AN EMOTIONAL DISORDER

DEPRESSION

- ❏ Feels sad
- ❏ Apathetic or lacks interest in previously pleasurable activities
- ❏ Socially isolative or withdrawn
- ❏ Pessimistic or hopeless
- ❏ Irritable
- ❏ Negative view of self
- ❏ Passive
- ❏ Lacks energy or always seems tired
- ❏ Somatic complaints
- ❏ Poor or excessive appetite
- ❏ Enuretic or encopretic
- ❏ Decreased school performance
- ❏ Poor concentration
- ❏ Reluctance to go to school
- ❏ Expresses suicidal thoughts or preoccupation with death

ANXIETY

- ❏ Excessive distress when separated from major caregivers
- ❏ Persistent worry
- ❏ Reluctance to attend school
- ❏ Somatic complaints
- ❏ Restless
- ❏ Irritable

❏ Poor concentration

❏ Easily fatigued

❏ Exaggerated startle response

❏ Hypervigilant

BEHAVIOR DISORDER

❏ Initiates fights

❏ Disobedient

❏ Defiant

❏ Destructive to property

❏ Bullies other children

❏ Argumentative

❏ Verbally hostile

❏ Disregards rules

❏ Conflicts with authority figures

❏ Resists directions

❏ Rebellious

❏ Engages in antisocial behavior (e.g., fire setting)

❏ Often truant

NOTE: For more criteria, see the American Psychiatric Association. (1994). *Diagnostic and statistical manual of mental disorders* (4th ed.). Washington, DC: Author.

PART II

Classroom Interactions and Interventions

3
LEARNING DISORDERS ARE ASSOCIATED WITH EMOTIONAL PROBLEMS

I was dyslexic . . . and I still have a hard time reading today. I remember vividly the pain and mortification I felt as a boy of 8 when I was assigned to read a short passage of a scripture with a community vesper service during the summer vacation in Maine—and did a thoroughly miserable job of it.

—Nelson Rockefeller
Former Vice President of
the United States
(Rockefeller, 1976)

School makes up a major portion of a child's life. Half of a child's waking hours are spent in school—learning, making friends, and developing an identity in the context of others—and school-related experiences dominate early development. Intuitively, it makes sense that if a child has significant struggles with learning—a major focus of early childhood—he or she will experience some consequences. In fact, research has shown that certain emotional problems are more frequently encountered in those who have learning disabilities. Having a learning disability may be a " 'risk factor' for the development of emotional problems" (Prout, Marcal, & Marcal, 1992, p. 62). Specifically, emotional problems may have resulted from attempts to cope with a learning disorder and repeated failures (Abrams, 1986; Chandler, 1994).

Learning disorders may also be strongly related to emotional problems, because the core deficits that interfere with learning affect social and emotional development (Bender & Wall, 1994). For example, a child with language processing problems will also probably have difficulty interacting in social situations in which language subtleties are important. Last, it may be that an underlying neurological abnormality is responsible for both learning and behavior problems (Spafford & Grosser, 1993). Although exactly what causes the emotional problems is unclear, it is hard to dismiss the substantial research findings that many children with learning disabilities also experience a number of social, emotional, and behavioral problems.

SELF-ESTEEM AND SELF-CONCEPT

The large body of research on self-esteem and self-concept in students with learning disabilities has yielded complicated findings. A substantial portion supports the idea that students with learning disabilities have worse self-concepts and lower self-esteem than their nondisabled peers and students with behavioral disorders (Grolnick & Ryan, 1990; Stanley, Dai, & Nolan, 1997). This may be due to the repeated failures experienced by children with learning disabilities (Meyer, 1983). Students with learning disabilities may also generalize from their deficits to an overall negative image of themselves (Heyman, 1990), perhaps because this tendency is shared by others. For example, Shauna, now a teenager, often complains that when people discover her reading disability, they talk slower and simplify their speech, "as if I were dumb." Some children may equate academic achievement with parental acceptance or self-competence, which produces feelings of inadequacy (Chandler, 1994). Despite her many sports trophies and musical accomplishments, 15-year-old Grace continues to report disappointment in herself for "not getting straight A's like my parents want." Poor self-concept may be related to hypersensitivity; children with learning disabilities tend to be fearful of further humiliation and become frustrated easily due to their repeated experiences of failure (Abrams, 1986; Short, 1992). This hypersensitivity played a role in Sam's reading problems, as featured in the case study below. Intelligence does not seem to prevent children with learning disabilities from adopting poor self-concepts and motivation and from experiencing negative emotional consequences such as depression. Students with learning disabilities who have very low levels of self-esteem and poor overall self-concepts may feel inadequate in academic, social, behavioral, and nonacademic skill areas (Kloomok & Cosden, 1994).

However, some research suggests that the extent of self-esteem difficulties may be limited. Some researchers have failed to find any significant differences in overall self-concept between students with learning disabilities and their nondisabled peers (Sabornie, 1994; Tollefson et al., 1982). It is not clear if this may be due to the ages of the children being researched. Interestingly, older youths and adolescents show less discrepancy than younger children, who perhaps have not yet developed adequate coping mechanisms. It may also be that children compensate with strengths in other areas, such as nonacademic abilities (Hagborg, 1996), or that academic ability is not as important to children with learning disabilities (Grolnick & Ryan, 1990).

Other researchers have found adequate overall self-concept but lower academic self-concept among youths with learning disabilities (Chapman, 1998; Heath, 1995). This may result from realistic views of their learning problems as being specific rather than reflecting a global lack of intelligence. High levels of perceived social support may also boost overall self-concept (Kloomok & Cosden, 1994). Even when a learning disability only affects academic self-concept, there is potential for compromised achievement. Children whose actual achievement suffers as a result of their poor self-concepts (and not just their learning disabilities) may create a self-fulfilling prophecy of poor school performance and learning, such as with Sam, featured in the case study that follows. Lower academic self-concepts are also related to children's lower academic expectations of future success (Hiebert, Wong, & Hunter, 1982).

Protecting the self-esteem and self-concept of students with learning disabilities may be accomplished in part by having a circumscribed view of learning disabilities instead of generalizing from one deficit area to overall competence and self-worth (Heyman, 1990; Kloomok & Cosden, 1994). This is important for both students and teachers. In our efforts to remediate and support children with learning disabilities, it is all too easy to forget that they also have unique talents and abilities that are unrelated to their disabilities. False assumptions—such as that a student who has a learning disability is less intelligent overall than his or her peers—may further contribute to the child's poor self-concept. Helping a child to understand "the specific nature and extent of a disability appears to be an important first step in accepting that disability, putting it into perspective and subsequently developing a positive self-concept" (Rothman & Cosden, 1995, p. 211). Reminding students of their uniqueness and intrinsic worth through stories such as *The Potter* and *The Special Flower* (both found at the end of this chapter) also reinforce positive self-concept.

Selective attention to positive feedback can also bolster self-esteem. Because students rely most heavily on feedback from their teachers to evaluate their performance (e.g., rather than comparisons to peers), favorable feedback from teachers may protect their self-esteem (Bear & Minke, 1996). Fostering success in areas not apparently directly related to school performance, such as body image and social relations, can also enhance a student's academic self-concept, since these areas have been found to be closely related (Hagborg, 1996).

✧ CASE STUDY: The Defensive Child

At first glance, Sam seemed to be a self-assured fifth grader—perhaps even too self-assured, as he could be argumentative, bossy, and obstinate. Over time, however, it became apparent that underneath Sam's tough exterior was a very sensitive child.

Sam had been diagnosed with a reading disability in second grade and had received remedial services ever since. His early diagnosis resulted primarily from the vigilance of his parents. Sam was their first child after two miscarriages, and they were especially doting. In addition to helping him with his homework, his parents took him to an after-school learning center three times a week and always enrolled him in a summer school program for dyslexic children. Despite their good intentions, Sam was keenly aware of his disability and felt as if he could never measure up to others' expectations. In the classroom, Sam easily became defensive when corrected by his teacher. He would often attempt to shift blame elsewhere. His classic response was to reply, "What about so-and-so's mistake?" He was also unwilling to admit mistakes and redo his work—hence his appearing oppositional. Sam could not tolerate any signs that he might be "flawed." In addition, he always seemed to need to be superior to his peers, bragging about himself or putting others down.

Sam's low self-esteem and overall negative self-concept was becoming increasingly problematic, because he began to refuse assistance and interventions for his reading disability. In effect, Sam was resisting what he perceived to be others' attempts to "fix" him. This was causing him to fall further behind, creating a vicious cycle of hypersensitivity and failure. His teachers were concerned about his need for reading support but were afraid to push it, because it only seemed to make him more resistant and isolated. For the time being, they decided to focus their efforts on addressing his self-esteem, in the hopes that a change in his view of himself would make him more accepting of remedial services. In addition, his primary teacher tried to make reading supports a natural part of her classroom, such as by pairing up students to read and asking students to tutor younger children. She hoped that if Sam did not feel singled out, he might be more receptive to building his reading abilities.

BUILDING SELF-ESTEEM

Because self-esteem is so fundamental to other areas of emotional well-being, interventions directed at building self-esteem are likely to have a strong impact. Taking a few minutes each day to build students' self-esteem will benefit all children, whether they have learning disabilities or not. Consider dedicating a bulletin board to be a "student showcase," where you can feature student accomplishments. By displaying various achievements, you demonstrate that a child who has raised his or her spelling test scores from 50% to 80% should be just as proud as another who did a kind deed or another who got an A on a report.

Modifying self-esteem interventions for children with learning disabilities may make them even more effective. Avoid actions that only highlight a child's deficits, rather than provide positive reinforcement. For example, when reminding children of their uniqueness, use examples that focus on nonacademic skills (e.g., "Irving always remembers to be polite"). Using the Guess Who I Am reproducible (found at the end of this chapter) is also an enjoyable way to build self-esteem, particularly if your school's Student of the Month is determined by academic accomplishments. You can feature one student per week, either by providing one clue each day or all at once (e.g., at Friday morning circle time). You can also assign one student to be the "interviewer" and another to be the featured student, as if they were a host and mystery guest on a television talk show. The purpose of the activity is to make individual children feel special and interesting outside their roles as a student and to help their fellow classmates see them in the same way.

Making students aware of the success of famous people who have had to deal with their learning disabilities can also be inspiring, suggesting that no matter how difficult their struggles are now, the potential for great futures is within reach. For example, growing up, Thomas Edison, the inventor, was thought to be stupid by both himself and his father. The renowned sculptor Auguste Rodin was labeled as "uneducable." Woodrow Wilson, former president of the United States, did not read until he was 11 years old (Thompson, 1971). Even Albert Einstein, a true genius, was told that "nothing good" would come of him (Patten, 1973). You may want to encourage older students with learning disabilities to profile these success stories for writing assignments (e.g., biographies).

DEPRESSION

Many researchers have found that students with learning disabilities experience more depression than their peers, though the rates of occurrence vary from 14% to 36% (Short, 1992; Stanley et al., 1997; Stevenson & Romney, 1984; Wright-Strawderman & Watson, 1992). Similarly, children referred to inpatient mental health centers for depression have a higher rate of learning disabilities than other nondepressed children referred for services (Kashani, Cantwell, Shekim, & Reid, 1982) and the general population (Fristad, Topolosky, Weller, & Weller, 1992). As with low self-esteem, younger children with learning disabilities may experience more severe depression than older children with learning disabilities (Wright-Strawderman & Watson, 1992). This may be because older children have increased understanding of their learning disabilities and can cope better (Hall & Haws, 1989).

There are many explanations for why children with learning disabilities might experience depression. Some children may not be able to tolerate the repeated frustration and failure they experience as a result of their learning disabilities. Their discouragement, if unchecked, can lead to feelings of helplessness, inadequacy, and hopelessness. Robbie, a third grader, seemed to be constantly sighing, angry at himself for his mistakes. In a moment of vulnerability, he once confided, "I wish I wasn't so bad at everything." Others may internalize criticism from others (e.g., people who have told them they are "lazy" or "stupid") and consequently develop self-hatred. Another possibility is that a child's learning disability has associated consequences that contribute to depression. For example, receiving pull-out services, being labeled, or otherwise being identified as different from their peers may increase children's sense of isolation. Actual peer rejection may follow, perhaps as a self-fulfilling prophecy. The type of learning disability may also make depression more likely. For example, core language deficits may interfere with social communication, leading to social problems and poor self-esteem. Nonverbal learning disabilities that involve social deficits and difficulty dealing with novelty may also be a particular risk factor for depression and suicidality because of social ostracism (Rourke, Young, & Leenars, 1989).

Depression in children with learning disabilities needs to be taken seriously, since suicidal feelings may occur. For example, in their study of 8- to 11-year-olds with learning disabilities, Wright-Strawderman and Watson (1992) found that 11% felt they wanted to kill themselves. Peck (1985) also found over a 3-year period in Los Angeles County that 50% of children under 15 years of age who committed suicide had been diagnosed with learning disabilities.

ANXIETY

Students with learning disabilities experience higher levels of overall anxiety than nondisabled students (Margalit & Zak, 1984; Rodriguez & Routh, 1989). It has been estimated that up to 25% of children with learning disabilities meet criteria for an anxiety disorder (Cantwell & Baker, 1991). This makes intuitive sense. Because children with learning disabilities face many situations during the school day where they might have trouble, their overall level of anticipatory anxiety may be high. Heightened anxiety may also be related to a student's sense that things are beyond his or her control (Margalit & Zak, 1984), since students with learning disabilities tend to see control over success and failure is in the hands of others (Grolnick & Ryan, 1990; Tarnowski & Nay, 1989). For example, Isabella, age 10, was constantly worrying that she would be "left behind" if her teacher did not help her with every task, since she had little confidence in her own ability to do well. Worrying about actual performance—such as after turning in an assignment—may also contribute to the anxiety of students with learning disabilities. These students may have a more difficult time recovering from their anxiety and stress as well (Dean & Rattan, 1987).

Students with learning disabilities may express their anxiety directly, such as by doubting themselves (e.g., "What if I fail the test?"). Anxiety can also be demonstrated more directly through somatic (physical) complaints (Margalit & Raviv, 1984). Children who "somaticize" their anxiety are unaware that they are worried and instead feel only the physical symptoms of anxiety (such as headaches, stomachaches, and fatigue). Some might think that these somatic complaints are made up to escape a task (e.g., being allowed to go to the nurse's room rather than do the math lesson). However, Margalit and Raviv (1984) found that children with learning disabilities were usually not permitted to leave the classroom for their somatic complaints. This suggests that somatic symptoms more likely communicate a child's distress and may be somewhat unconscious attempts to elicit support from others.

DEALING WITH DEPRESSION
AND ANXIETY

Children who experience depression and anxiety as a consequence of their learning disabilities need help changing their negative mind-sets. Encouraging students to have a realistic view of their circumscribed disabilities, and not to overgeneralize, is also a good approach. One way to facilitate this is to have students reflect on their strengths and weaknesses. Instead of asking them to identify what they are good or bad at, however, it is more helpful to ask them to complete the sentence "I am better at _____ than I am at _____." This communicates that weaknesses are relative and are not fixed traits. The spirit of the activity is not only to model acceptance of one's limitations but to teach children how to grow and learn from their mistakes. This helps them to avoid "catastrophizing" their problems, or making their struggles worse than they actually are.

You can also address depression and anxiety by being realistic. It does not help to say, "Don't worry, you'll do fine," unless you can provide some kind of evidence to back this up. Reassurance such as "You've studied really hard. I think you'll do well on the test" is more believable.

Older children can benefit from reasoning that challenges the beliefs underlying their depression and anxiety. If a student laments, "No one likes me," or worries that he or she will be ostracized, ask why. Gently point out inconsistencies (e.g., "You said no one likes you, but Jamie wanted to be your reading partner") to shift his or her thinking to a more accurate appraisal of themselves and others.

INTERPERSONAL RELATIONSHIPS
AND LONELINESS

In general, students with learning disabilities report more problems in interpersonal relationships and are seen as being less socially competent than their nondisabled peers (Bryan, 1974; Roberts & Zubrick, 1993). Specifically, they may use less assertive and effective conversational behaviors (Wojnilower & Gross, 1988) and may actually misread nonverbal communication (Bryan, 1977). Students with learning disabilities tend to rate themselves negatively on social acceptance (Heath & Wiener, 1996) and also report more frequent victimization by their peers (Sabornie, 1994). In addition, passivity, which often accompanies learning disabilities, may hinder development of positive peer relationships (Margalit & Raviv, 1984; Wong & Wong, 1980). Overall, students with learning disabilities appear to be more likely to experience more peer rejection (Swanson & Malone, 1992).

Given their often impaired social relationships, you might expect that students with learning disabilities report more loneliness than students without learning disabilities (Margalit & Levin-Alyagon, 1994; Sabornie, 1994). In part, this may be due to an awareness of their real social difficulties (Tur-Kaspa, Weisel, & Segev, 1998) or may reflect a subjective sense of isolation from others because they feel different. Students may also feel lonely because they are less integrated than their peers as a result of participation in special classes or remedial pull-out services (Sabornie, 1994). Imagine being the last one to a social gathering every day, knowing that you missed out on an hour of something but not knowing what. Understandably, you might feel left out or feel like an outsider. Perhaps because of repeated rejection by peers, students with learning disabilities also may have greater expectation of loneliness in the future (Tur-Kaspa et al., 1998).

Classroom social relationships are an important part of a child's life, particularly if the child has learning disabilities, because they impact self-esteem and other areas of emotional well-being. Building Relationships and Reducing Isolation (found at the end of this chapter) will give you some ideas.

AGGRESSION AND DISRUPTIVE BEHAVIOR

Researchers debate whether learning disabilities specifically cause aggression and disruptive behavior or if they are only indirectly related. Some believe that learning disabilities directly cause juvenile delinquency (Crealock, 1986), perhaps because they contribute to a cycle of frustration, failure, limited skills, and restricted future opportunities. Specifically, school failure may lead to future antisocial behavior because youth are unable to meet their goals legally (Farrington, 1995). However, the majority of research does not strongly support this (see Williams & McGee, 1994). What has been found is that learning disabilities and problem behavior, such as police contact in adolescence, coexist at high rates. Cornwall and Bawden (1992) reviewed research on the causal relationship between reading disorders (the most commonly diagnosed learning disability) and aggression. They concluded that specific reading disabilities do not lead to aggressive or delinquent behavior. However, "reading disabled boys during early schooling do appear to be at higher risk of later conduct disorder," perhaps because the "roots of delinquency" can be found in the behavioral problems that often accompany learning disabilities (Williams & McGee, 1994, p. 455). Underlying cognitive and neuropsychological deficits, such as poor verbal, reasoning, and problem-solving skills, may also contribute to an impulsive behavioral style, which affects social maturity and the likelihood of aggressive behavior (Seguin, Pihl, Harden, Tremblay & Boulerice, 1995).

Learning disorders can also interfere with the child's interpretation of social cues. For example, oppositional children tend to interpret ambiguous situations as containing more threat and consequently respond with aggression (Dodge, 1986). In a similar fashion, a child with learning problems (particularly in attention to and interpretation of nonverbal social cues, for example) may interpret an ambiguous situation as threatening and display defensive behavior (such as verbal hostility or a preemptive physical strike) that is actually unnecessary but triggers an argument or fight (Seguin, Boulerice, Harden, Tremblay, & Pihl, 1999).

Poor verbal skills may also lead to aggressive behavior. Not being able to negotiate, to verbally deescalate a situation, or even to apologize appropriately can all result in an altercation. Physical release may be sought if one cannot verbally express frustration. Although it does not appear that learning disabilities consistently cause hyperactivity (Chadwick, Taylor, Heptinstall, & Danckaerts, 1999), deficits in executive functioning, such as in regulation of arousal and attention, can also contribute to disruptive behavior. Learning problems may also contribute to a child's sense of isolation, which may lead to embitterment and a desire to seek physical revenge. Children who feel threatened but cannot defend themselves verbally may resort to physical means.

One cannot (and should not) predict aggressive or disruptive behavior from the mere presence of learning disabilities. However, for some children, and in some situations where other stressors such as economic disadvantage exist, learning disabilities can join with other factors to result in externalizing behavior problems. Given enough frustration, disappointment, peer rejection, and self-hatred, a child may lash out at others, particularly those who most strongly elicit these feelings. An important distinction is that in this scenario, the learning disorder (i.e., cognitive deficit) itself does not cause disruptive behavior, but rather, the associated emotional consequences and poor coping skills may lead to acting-out behavior. The following case study illustrates how aggression can stem from problems related to learning disabilities.

✧ CASE STUDY: **The Acting-Out Student**

What was most striking about Maria was her anger. Although she was just beginning third grade, she seemed to have stored up enough rage for a lifetime. It wasn't uncommon for her to arrive at school in a bad mood, to have an angry outburst before lunch, and to leave school seeming ready to explode. On her good days, she could be diffused with some compassion and a time-out. On her bad days, she spent more time in the principal's office than in her classroom.

Prior to being diagnosed with a mixed receptive-expressive language disorder, Maria had tried to pass through the school day undetected. Though she often had appeared sullen, by no means was she aggressive. After her diagnosis, concerted efforts were made to build her language skills. Unfortunately, this seemed only to increase Maria's frustration, as she was repeatedly challenged to the limits of her language abilities, both at home and school. Maria seemed to resent the extra attention her learning problems created. She was no longer just a "quiet child" or "in her own world," but someone who "needs special help." Maria's behavior took a turn for the worse. To release her resentment and frustration, she began resorting to physical expressions, since she had difficulty expressing her thoughts verbally. It began with throwing tantrums, then progressed to throwing books and school materials, and even developed into striking out at peers. Maria's low frustration tolerance made it difficult to predict what would set her off. Typically, a series of little disappointments would build until she could no longer tolerate her failures, resulting in an outward display of anger grossly out of proportion to the triggering event.

REDUCING AGGRESSIVE AND DISRUPTIVE BEHAVIOR

Serious aggression and disruptive behavior, whether it is related to a learning disorder or not, should not be tolerated in the classroom, and discipline according to your school policies should be implemented. Minor incidents (e.g., yelling) also require consequences (e.g., loss of privileges). Consider whether the actions are due to learning disabilities, however. For example, a visually impaired student was once sent to the principal's office for interrupting another class during testing. His behavior was not malicious; rather, he was physically unable to see the sign on the door announcing that testing was occurring. In the same way, if disruptive behavior has occurred because of the nature of the child's learning disability, use the incident as a chance to talk privately with the child about the impact of his or her learning disability, rather than provide punishment.

If you believe that the acting-out was an expression of pent-up frustration over learning struggles, discipline is still appropriate. At the same time, follow up with instruction on healthier ways of coping. (Suggestions for building coping skills can be found in Chapter 6.) Early recognition of triggers for acting-out can also help to prevent outbursts. For example, if you know that reading lessons are usually stressful for your student with dyslexia, proactively address the child with comments such as "Tell me if you are feeling frustrated, and I'll help you." You may be able to diffuse frustration with a quick pep talk.

Promoting self-control also contributes to decreased aggression. By praising children's compliance and attributing it to their good intentions, you reinforce the notion that they are in charge of their own behavior (Bergin & Bergin, 1999). For example, when an angry child finally does calm down, you can say, "Good job calming yourself. I know you want to be in control and that you don't want to hurt other people."

Classroom management strategies that you have learned during your training are also helpful. You can find excellent ideas in books such as *Behavior Management: A Practical Approach for Educators* by James Walker and Thomas Shea.

GETTING HELP

Perhaps the best way to minimize the social, behavioral, and emotional problems associated with learning disabilities is to address the learning disabilities directly. Providing appropriate remedial and support services is essential and is best done in collaboration with learning specialists. Strengthening compensatory abilities is also important. For example, a child with a math disability but strong visual memory may be able to compensate for poor knowledge of multiplication facts by visualizing a "times table." Beyond this, however, specific interventions (such as those described in this chapter) aimed at possible areas of difficulty should be implemented.

If you try these and other interventions and find that your students' emotional or behavior problems are still too much to handle and are interfering with their achievement, refocus your energy on getting outside help. Supportive counseling, therapy, and even medication may not only be appropriate but may be required to enable a student to work on his or her learning problems. A referral to your school-based support team for evaluation may be in order.

SUMMARY

Research has linked learning disabilities to a number of social, emotional and behavioral problems. Low self-esteem, depression, anxiety, loneliness, and aggression have all been found to exist at higher rates among children with learning disabilities, though it is unclear whether learning disorders directly or indirectly cause these troubles. In addition to formal support services (e.g., special education), you can take steps to minimize these problems in your students with learning disabilities. Building self-esteem by focusing on the whole person and showcasing nonacademic talents is helpful. Depression and anxiety can be reduced by changing the negative thoughts that perpetuate worry and self-pity. Aggressive and disruptive behavior can also be decreased by addressing the triggers for acting out. As a teacher, you also have an important role in building friendships among your students to safeguard against isolation.

Story Time: The Potter

Marianne was an excellent potter. The townspeople loved to buy what she created from clay, because each object came out so beautifully with her special touch. One day, Marianne decided to make a vase for herself. She wanted to make a special vase that was unlike any other and would be beautiful no matter what flowers were placed in it.

Early one morning, Marianne arose and began to shape the clay on her potter's wheel. At first, everything was going fine, and she grew more and more excited that she would soon have the most beautiful vase ever. Then her finger slipped, and suddenly, the clay began to twist and turn on her potter's wheel, leaving a bumpy shape. Try as she might, she couldn't fix it. What was supposed to be a beautiful tall vase was now short, too wide, and uneven. Marianne decided to put it aside and to start over the next day.

The next morning, Marianne set out again to make her vase. The same thing happened. Her fingers slipped, and this time, instead of a round bottom to the vase, the bottom was sort of square, causing the whole vase to look lopsided. Disappointed, she gave up and decided to try once more the next day.

For the next 3 days, Marianne kept making mistakes, and each day, she grew more and more upset. By the end of the week, Marianne had five pieces of pottery that looked nothing like the vase she wanted. As she stood in her shop trying to figure out what to do with the mess she had made, her friend the baker came in. "How can I help you today?" she asked. The baker replied, "I am looking for a gift for my mother and hope you can help me. I have searched everywhere for something different and special for her." As he spoke, his eyes lit up. "There it is," he exclaimed, "What a beautiful mixing bowl—it's perfect; she loves to cook!" Marianne was puzzled—she hadn't made any mixing bowls. Then she realized that the baker had seen her first failed attempt at a vase—the short, wide, bumpy one. The baker seemed so happy, she didn't tell him that it wasn't a mixing bowl, but an ugly vase. Instead, she wrapped it up and sent him on his way.

Just then, her neighbor came in. "I'm desperate," she sighed. "I have searched all over and I can't find a present for my daughter." As the neighbor looked around the shop, her eye caught Marianne's second failed attempt. "My! What a pretty open box," she laughed. "My daughter would love to have this to put her CDs in! I should have come here first. I'll take it." Strangely enough, that day Marianne sold all five misshapen vases, and each time, the customer thought it was the perfect gift, even though none of them thought they were vases. Marianne realized that even though she still didn't have the perfect vase, she had made five other perfect gifts for her friends.

People are like pottery—each one is different from the other. Just as a mixing bowl shouldn't try to be a vase, so you shouldn't try to be something you are not just to please someone. Each person is valuable for who they are, and each of us is just the person we were meant to be.

Story Time: The Special Flower

Dr. Sumi loved flowers. She had flowers growing in her garden, flowers in vases around her house, pictures of flowers on her walls, dishes shaped like flowers, and flowers on her clothes. She even had glasses that looked like flowers! Dr. Sumi was a botanist, and her job was to find out about different flowers. She searched all over the world for beautiful flowers. When she found one, she would have a big party to celebrate and invite all of her friends to see it.

Every day, Dr. Sumi would put on her hat and gloves and go searching for flowers. Usually, she saw flowers she already knew about, but she was always excited to see them. One day, something caught her eye. It was the most beautiful flower she had ever seen. She was sure that no one else had ever seen it before, and she couldn't believe how lucky she was to find this special flower. She carefully brought it home to show the other scientists.

Imagine her surprise when her friends started laughing! "What kind of flower is that," they cried, "it looks so funny! Why, it doesn't even look like a flower!" Dr. Sumi knew why they were laughing. The color of the flower was different, sort of like red, yellow, green, and purple all mixed together. It was square on one side, pointy on the other, had a circle in the center, and a long bumpy thing sticking out of it. It was huge, but the stem and leaves were very tiny. Most of all, if it got wet, it smelled like scrambled eggs. "It may not look like anything you have seen before," she said, "but that's why I love it. There is no flower like this in the whole entire world—nothing even comes close to it." Her friends stopped laughing. Dr. Sumi continued, "I have searched my whole life for something so precious. I am going to give it the special attention it deserves." And with that, Dr. Sumi did an amazing thing. She started taking down the pictures of flowers in her house, gave away the flowers in her yard, put away her dishes shaped like flowers, and even got new glasses that didn't look like flowers. She told everyone, "This flower is the most special flower in the world, because it is the only one like it. This is what I have been looking for."

Each of you is like Dr. Sumi's special flower, because there is only one person in the entire universe like you. You can search near and far, across the oceans and deserts, up in the mountains and down in the valleys, and you will never find another person just like you. Maybe you think you look funny or don't act like other people or can't do things like other people can. What makes you different from other people is what makes you special, special enough to be treated as if you were the only person in the whole wide world.

GUESS WHO I AM

A funny thing I can do is . . .

My favorite food is . . .

After school, I like to . . .

When I grow up, I want to be a . . .

One special thing about me is . . .

BUILDING RELATIONSHIPS AND REDUCING ISOLATION

Rationale: Studies have shown that the most effective way to build relationships and overcome divisive attitudes between groups is to engage individuals in common goal-oriented activities (Sherif, Harvey, White, Hood, & Sherif, 1961). By encouraging children to work together, you help them to overlook alienating differences and to form positive working relationships. The following activities all entail students working together toward a common goal. In the process, they learn how similar they are to each other and encounter positive qualities in each other.

Ideas:

♦ Develop a class logo, motto, or mascot by which you can establish a shared identity.

♦ Divide students into pairs or small groups (be sure to make the groups diverse), where each group completes a part of a puzzle. Join all groups to finish the puzzle. Provide various rewards for finishing within a certain time limit or demonstrating good cooperation. (Make sure you have completed the puzzle first so you can divide it appropriately!)

♦ Create a class project to benefit the school or a particular person, such as producing a surprise "Happy Birthday" mural for another teacher.

♦ Begin a friendship ritual. Just before lunch each day, ask students to raise their hands or line up according to similarities, such as the number of siblings, favorite foods, and so forth. Make a point to comment on any similarities between children who have a difficult relationship.

♦ Reward cooperation, particularly among students who do not get along well. For example, assign a troubled pair to accomplish a certain task that requires joint effort, such as rearranging books in alphabetical order within a certain time frame. If they succeed, reward the pair with a special privilege (e.g., eating lunch in your room) and the class with free play time.

EMOTIONAL PROBLEMS CAN HIDE LEARNING DISABILITIES

etting expectations has a lot to do with
a lot of learning disabled people I know.
If [we can get] people [to] set their expectations lower,
we can get by better. It's unfortunate, but it gets you by.

—Nick
College student with dyslexia
(Barga, 1996)

One common interaction between learning disabilities and emotional/behavioral disorders is that the symptoms of emotional disturbance overshadow learning disabilities. This often happens when a child's emotional disorder has already been identified, since it provides a ready explanation for the child's problems. It also occurs when the child's demeanor and actions command attention, such as when they are disruptive to the class. Some researchers have found that students with significant reading problems also had been rated as more hyperactive and aggressive upon entering school (McGee, Williams, Share, Anderson, & Silva, 1986), suggesting that emotional problems can hide learning disabilities from a very early age. Furthermore, some emotional conditions include symptoms that resemble learning disabilities, making it easier to excuse a child's learning difficulties. For example, slowed thinking, poor memory, and inadequate concentration may occur with depression as well as with learning disabilities. Thus, even though a teacher may be capable of identifying a possible learning disorder, it may go unnoticed because a child's emotional concerns are more salient.

THE TEACHER'S ROLE

Some emotional problems can be quite dramatic in their presentation. For example, aggression, acting out, and other disruptive behaviors often present significant classroom management problems. Because dealing with disruptive students is perhaps the greatest source of stress for teachers (Montalvo, Bair, & Boor, 1995), your attention may be justifiably focused on the emotional problems a student displays in your classroom, not only for the individual child's welfare but also for the benefit of his or her peers (not to mention your own sanity). Other emotional conditions, such as depression and anxiety, may not create classroom management problems but may nevertheless grab your attention. Children who appear insecure, frightened, overwhelmed, or lonely pull at the heartstrings of their teachers, who may spend extra effort to comfort and support them.

It is admirable to pay attention to students' emotional problems and to try to do something about them. However, it is important to make sure that a child's emotional problems do not overshadow everything else. When we begin to make excuses for children's poor academic performance (e.g., "He's just having a hard time because of the divorce") or when we overlook learning problems because of the magnitude of the emotional and behavioral concerns (e.g., "Her real problem is not math—it's that she has such a bad temper"), we need to evaluate whether we have allowed emotional problems to overshadow other needs the child may have. In the following case study, Megan's well-intentioned teacher focused almost exclusively on Megan's emotional needs, causing her learning disability to be undetected for a period of time.

❖ CASE STUDY: The Withdrawn Child

When Megan entered my second-grade classroom, I thought she was quite shy and reserved. She would not initiate any interactions with me, and also avoided her peers. Megan was very passive, never drawing attention to herself, and only responding when I directly questioned her. As the school year continued,

Megan seemed to become less engaged, instead of being more comfortable in the classroom setting, as the other children did. I asked around and found out that Megan had an older brother in a special education class for students with severe disabilities. I assumed that Megan was living in the shadow of her brother's needs, and tried to reach out to her with words of encouragement and special tasks, such as letting her be my assistant for the day. Unfortunately, nothing seemed to change. Megan actually seemed to become more timid and to fall further behind the other children. She stopped turning in her homework, often did not finish her in-class assignments, and resisted giving responses, even when I called on her.

At this point, I thought that Megan was probably depressed, so I discussed my concerns about Megan's possible depression with the school-based support team. They felt a comprehensive assessment of her situation could be helpful. In the process of the evaluation, it was discovered that Megan had significant problems with memory. They suggested that her emotional problems, like being overwhelmed and withdrawn, were worse when she was required to act independently, such as when she needed to remember task directions to complete a task. The more I thought about that, the more it made sense. For example, being the teacher's assistant is a morale booster for most children, but for Megan it was painful, because she had trouble remembering the other students' names, and she couldn't pass out folders and papers correctly. When I looked inside Megan's desk, I discovered an enormous stack of untouched homework sheets. Apparently, she hadn't remembered to take them home. As I thought back over the fall, I noticed that Megan's deteriorating performance and behavior seemed to coincide with a gradual shift to a more independent and student-driven class schedule. I had been encouraging my students to take initiative to use centers, to complete supplemental projects on their own, and to follow through on assignments discussed at the beginning of the school day. All of this must have been overwhelming to Megan.

In Megan's case, it is very likely that her underlying memory difficulties, as well as her potentially difficult home situation, resulted in feelings of depression. Megan's primary method of coping was to withdraw, hoping perhaps that if she could fade into the background, little would be required of her. Because her emotional problems were so immediately apparent, the sympathetic teacher's initial efforts were to provide support and comfort. Only after searching for underlying causes were Megan's significant memory deficits recognized and addressed with specific interventions.

THE STUDENT'S ROLE

Just as it is entirely possible that students' learning problems are overlooked by their teachers because of the severity of their emotional issues, students may also be more focused on their emotional experiences and may be unaware of their learning disability. In particular, most younger children cannot explain, "I'm upset, because I don't understand this, and I don't know what to do." Instead, they may protest about how "stupid" the task is or may act out in frustration. Victor, featured in the following case study, provides an example of how behavior problems may disguise a learning disability. Children may not be able to figure out the reasons for their emotions and simply feel very agitated, restless, or uncomfortable without knowing why. Naturally, if a student does not report any learning struggles, and the teacher is occupied with managing the child's emotional displays, it will be difficult to identify the underlying learning disorder.

It may also be difficult to identify a learning disability, because children develop natural compensatory mechanisms to try to hide their troubles. One constellation of these coping methods is specifically related to academics. For example, children may rely on their relatively strong memory ability to disguise a reading problem. One child made up for her problems in reading comprehension by using her imagination to make up elaborate story endings and fantastical responses to questions. Another devised a clever way of multiplying that entailed constructing lengthy tables and number lists for each numeral. A busy teacher may not notice these compensatory behaviors, especially if students are successful in their creative approaches and able to identify the correct responses to questions. Such cleverness may be a sign of brilliance or may signal a hidden area of weakness.

Another possibility is that children intentionally try to shift attention to something other than their learning problems. This is probably what was happening to Ricky, portrayed in the "Class Clown" case study that follows. Children quickly learn what gets attention and can be purposeful in drawing attention if it relieves anxiety in other areas. For example, children will act out to stop their parents from fighting, because they have found that their behavioral problems are a successful diversion. Similarly, Abrams (1986) describes a child who " 'willed herself to think about a million different things' whenever it was time for a reading lesson and the inevitable pain of failure" (p. 193). Not only was she distracting herself, but it is likely that she also distracted her teacher from her reading difficulties by appearing so inattentive.

Children may also intentionally behave in ways to hide their learning disabilities. For example, Karen "knew precisely at what point to excuse herself from the class to use the bathroom and thus avoid having to read aloud" (Barga, 1996, p. 419). Children may also cheat to hide their learning disabilities, such as by watching a movie for a book report or copying answers from other classmates. Thus, in various ways, children can hinder the discovery of their learning disabilities by others. The following case illustrations demonstrate the possibility of children's emotional conditions hiding learning problems.

❖ CASE STUDY: The Volatile Child

Victor, a first grader, was well-known throughout the school despite his young age. In kindergarten, he had so exasperated his teacher that he was the subject of many lunchtime conversations in the teachers' lounge. There was the time when he suddenly burst out of his classroom, running up two flights of stairs to visit his fifth-grade cousin. No one could forget the story about how he kicked the teacher's aide while in line for the bus at the end of the day. Many behavioral interventions were tried during that year with little success. Meetings with his mother and grandmother also had not been successful in curbing Victor's disruptive behavior, in part due to mutual animosity. School staff expressed concern about child neglect when Victor came to school in the winter dressed only in shorts and a T-shirt, explaining that he couldn't find any other clothes to wear. Everyone hoped that the school social worker would be able to make some headway. If not, perhaps he would "grow out of it" with time.

Unfortunately, now that he was in first grade, Victor seemed to be in even less control. Worse, he often seemed more than just hyperactive. He seemed overly sensitive and hostile to his teachers and, at times, even to his peers. Time-outs, removal of recess privileges, and tokens for good behavior seemed to have little impact. His first-grade teacher found herself commiserating with Victor's kindergarten teacher during lunchtimes and being haunted by his name (which she seemed to use so frequently), even in her sleep. Feeling that she had exhausted all of her classroom management resources, Victor's teacher decided to refer him for a special education evaluation, hoping that perhaps he could receive counseling services if found to have emotional disturbance (ED).

During the course of the evaluation, intelligence testing revealed that although Victor's language skills were age-appropriate, his mathematics abilities were quite deficient. When the school psychologist pressed him with additional math questions, Victor became very angry, throwing the testing materials to the ground, yelling, and attempting to flee the room. It seemed that Victor was unable to tolerate his difficulties in math, in part because his overall sense of self-worth was quite fragile. Adopting a "tough front" not only made him feel less vulnerable but also displayed his anger at being made to feel stupid and rejected by his peers and family. Unfortunately, his aggressive stance also alienated his teachers and delayed his receiving the remedial assistance he required for his math disability.

✦ CASE STUDY: **The Class Clown**

Ricky, a fourth grader, was generally a popular kid. He was a natural leader, which could be unfortunate, given the fact that he often led his peers away from the task at hand. Ricky loved to make jokes, and his loud booming voice derailed many a lesson. Ricky's clowning around was not limited to playing jokes on others or teasing other children; he also told self-deprecatory jokes, with a very common refrain being "Oh, I forgot . . . AGAIN!" His antics were generally amusing, and although they required some behavior management, he was not aggravating by any means. He just seemed to thrive on the attention that his peers gave him (as well as appearing delighted when his teacher laughed at his shenanigans). Ricky wasn't a particularly good student. His teacher often commented, "If you would stop making jokes, Ricky, you might actually learn something."

When his behaviors became increasingly disruptive and more frequent, however, it was apparent that there was more going on than his goofing around suggested. Ricky had significantly underdeveloped reading abilities. In fact, he had struggled with reading as far back as kindergarten, when he had great difficulty learning the letters of the alphabet and their corresponding sounds. Because of his infectious personality, however, his teachers had generally

(continued)

❖ CASE STUDY: Continued

brushed aside his reading problems, believing that he "just wasn't applying himself" or that he wasn't giving his full attention to reading because of his social preoccupations. His written assignments were sloppy, with many spelling errors, but again his teachers assumed that he was simply rushing to finish the tasks and was "careless." For Ricky, however, he had found a way to gain positive attention, feel good about himself, and get through the school day without being paralyzed by his reading disorder.

UNCOVERING COEXISTING LEARNING DISABILITIES

With any child who is experiencing or displaying difficulties in the classroom, it is important to have a broad perspective on what may be happening. When problems persist beyond a particular incident, you should consider the possibility that multiple factors may be at work to create a disturbance in the child's functioning. Several areas should be investigated—initially as a sort of checklist for possibilities and more thoroughly as warranted by the initial screening. When the child's emotional state or behavioral change is a primary concern, systematically proceeding through the following steps can help clarify the factors contributing to the current problems. Using the Behavior Analysis worksheet at the end of this chapter may also be helpful.

First, attempt to identify what the specific problem is. Use the Behavior Analysis worksheet to examine the behavior. What may get your attention most is when children hit their peers. However, the "problem" may not be aggression but a more general underlying issue. For example, children who strike out at anything nearby when they encounter difficulty or are somehow frustrated (e.g., throwing things, pushing things off their desk, and so forth) may have an underlying emotional/behavioral issue of low frustration tolerance. By the time the aggressive acts are observed, students may be several steps removed from the underlying issue.

Second, trace the occurrence of the emotional display or behaviors and identify when they were first noticed. This may be anything from a gut feeling that something is wrong with a child to a clear time marker (e.g., the week after winter break). Sometimes, it may be quite difficult to identify the initial occurrence, but your earliest recollection of the problem, even if it was not the onset, can be helpful in understanding what is happening with your student. It is also helpful to talk with other teachers and support personnel to get their perspectives on when the problems began. For example, the lunchroom monitor or gym teacher may have noticed some behavioral problems before they became apparent in the classroom.

Next, consider the factors that may be affecting the situation. It is best to use a brainstorming approach to this step, in which you generate as many factors as possible before evaluating them. Consider factors related to the child's world, such as their home and family, peers, developmental stage, and any significant recent experiences or stressors. Recent topics of conversation or focus in their sharing time and writing may also provide clues. For example, perhaps children have been complaining about not having enough time to complete assignments and are anxious about their "slowness" in comparison to their peers' or your expectations. Think about any compensatory behavior that a child may be displaying, such as cheating on spelling tests or frequent requests to change or substitute assignments.

Consider the classroom environment: recent changes to the class schedule or physical environment, current content being taught (particularly in comparison to the demands of content taught previously), the climate of the classroom and peers' responses to the individual, and when the behaviors occur relative to what is happening in the classroom. You may notice, for example, that the worst behavioral problems occur in the late morning—typically the time you do writing exercises.

Last, consider factors related to you as a teacher: your responses to the student, your expectations for him or her, the extent to which you are bothered by the student and other reactions you may have, your attempts to remedy the situation, and any similar experiences with the problem in other children or in the past. This last area of self-evaluation is particularly important, because it can reveal insights that help to clarify the child's difficulties. For example, if you find that you become very frustrated and discouraged, to the point of feeling that anything you do to try to change the child or situation will be useless, it is probably safe to assume that the child's emotional and behavioral concerns have become too overwhelming and may be limiting your perspective on the situation. We all have pet peeves, and we cannot realistically believe that we will be fond of every student we will teach. You may become aware that your frustration tolerance for this child is particularly low (e.g., but not for another student who has similar problems). You may also realize that you have not been interested in attempting interventions suggested by others. Feelings such as these are signs that you need to talk with others (who are not as fed up as you may be) to get a more objective perspective on what is happening with your student.

Assuming that you have gone through the above steps, it may still be difficult to identify the reasons behind the child's emotional and behavioral problems. It is important, therefore, to thoroughly investigate the child's academic performance. Suppose your student has been easily angered ever since spring break. You recall that it was after this vacation that she suddenly began doing poorly on math assignments. Looking back at your lesson plan book, you note that concepts of place value were introduced around that time. Perhaps the child's conceptual struggles are resulting in the recent emotional displays. If the achievement problems are not circumscribed to a subject area, consider whether they are related to a particular skill area, such as writing. Exceedingly poor handwriting skills, for example, may result in oppositionality any time significant writing is required. Perhaps the academic problems are not specifically related to subjects or skills but require similar metacognitive or processing skills. For instance, a child's mood changes and overall decline in performance may have begun around the time that a new classroom homework policy was implemented, and are reflective of the child's global difficulties in planning, tracking, and organizing.

This systematic process should give you several kinds of information that will indicate whether a learning disability may be present in addition to emotional and behavioral problems. You will have gotten a sense of the child's academic strengths and weaknesses and any sensitivities to different learning and teaching styles. You will have ruled out (or in) other factors in the child's life that may be producing the current problems. You will have also evaluated your own role in the current situation.

INTERVENTION

Poor school performance and behavioral problems often go hand-in-hand (Thompson, Lampron, Johnson, & Eckstein, 1990). It is important to avoid an either-or perspective, in which a child's problems are explained as either an emotional/behavioral problem or as a learning disability. Rather, the likelihood that both exist is strong. It is crucial that one area not be overlooked because of the salience of the other.

When you have deduced that a child's emotional or behavioral issues have hidden a learning problem, the first priority should be to obtain appropriate remedial and support services. Refer the student for a comprehensive evaluation. Uncovering how the learning disability has affected the child's learning is essential. For example, has the student failed to acquire basic reading skills, which has prevented him or her from learning in other content areas? Establishing some sense of the student's potential abilities, usually apparent through the course of a psychoeducational evaluation, is important for goal setting for remedial services.

Helping children understand the link between the learning disability and the behaviors you have observed is the next step. This is especially important if they were unaware of or unable to identify their own struggles with learning. Take time to explain the nature of the learning deficits. Having the student understand the learning disability is essential to overcoming it at an early age. Express understanding for their emotional reactions and previous ways of coping. This will enable the child to gain maximum benefit from your interventions. For example, suppose the student has dyslexia but has been told that she is lazy and stupid. You can join the child's parents in approaching the child about the learning disability, so you are all working from the same perspective. A simple explanation to give for dyslexia is that the child hears sounds differently than other people, and that this makes learning, particularly reading, confusing. Tell the student she will get help so that reading will not be as difficult and learning will be more fun, but be realistic. Acknowledge that it will take a lot of effort and cooperation on the child's part. Be sure to point out that the outcome will be worth the effort.

Next, focus on building the child's coping skills. The fact that the student got your attention with emotional or behavioral problems suggests that she is unable to adequately cope with her learning problems. Emphasize the importance of expressing and dealing with frustration in a healthy manner. Encourage the student to seek out help and support appropriately. Consider developing a special sign to be used just between the two of you—a quick gesture like thumbs up—to communicate when a child is feeling distressed or needs encouragement. This simple act can have great impact. It not only solidifies your relationship as supportive and special, but it provides assistance with some degree of privacy for the child, who may feel embarrassed about being different.

Treating emotional expression as a natural part of being a community is also helpful. Simple ways to do this are to identify emotions in yourself and others as they occur, noting facial expressions and other signs of a person's feeling state. For example, you might explain, "I'm not thinking clearly because I'm frustrated and tired. Let me do that a bit later after I've taken a break." Labeling your students' feelings and encouraging them to do the same is also important. If a child is clearly angry, for example, you might say, "You seem very mad. You have a scowl on your face, and I just saw you throw your book bag."

Alternatively, you can implement this with your entire class by using "mood markers," such as those found in the worksheets at the end of this chapter. (Use the bears for younger children; older children may prefer the symbols representing feelings.) This not only helps others respond to them more appropriately, but it also helps children to be attuned to their own emotions. A child can simply place a mood marker on his or her desk to indicate their mood and need for support and can remove it when it is no longer necessary. Helping children recognize and express their emotions appropriately reduces the likelihood that the feelings will build up and result in acting out or in depressive and anxiety disorders. Also, it raises the possibility that they will have the internal resources to deal with their learning challenges. In addition, introduce the student to age-appropriate coping methods, such as journaling, taking rest breaks, breaking tasks into smaller parts, and rewarding themselves for accomplishing a goal.

It may be helpful to encourage the child to set personal goals, since it is likely that a flood of intervention may feel imposed from the outside and may result in passivity. My Personal Project, the reproducible worksheet at the end of this chapter, can be used for this purpose. Help children identify one behavior or learning problem they are motivated to work on (it may not be the same as yours) and have them commit to working on it for an age-appropriate period (e.g., one month for upper grades). This starts the student off in a proactive mind-set that will be crucial to overcoming the learning disability.

Last, if you feel that the child's emotional and behavioral problems have become too unmanageable for the child or for your classroom, get help from school support personnel, such as school psychologists, counselors, and social workers. Formal intervention for their emotional and behavioral problems is essential to children's being able to tackle their learning problems, as well as for your mental health and ability to help them.

SUMMARY

Both you and your student may unintentionally allow emotional and behavioral issues to overshadow learning problems. Uncovering hidden learning disabilities requires a thorough investigation of the multiple factors that are contributing to the problems you have noticed. Once a learning difficulty has been discovered, formal intervention (e.g., special education referral) should take place. In addition, you can aid your students by providing a simple explanation of the learning disability, by building their coping methods, and by helping them set personal goals for their behavior and/or achievement.

BEHAVIOR ANALYSIS WORKSHEET

What is the behavior problem?

When does it occur?

How many times a day does it occur?

What happens before the behavior?

How do you usually deal with the behavior?

What happens after the behavior?

Does the student receive any unintended benefit as a result of the behavior (e.g., peer attention, avoiding a task)?

AM I OVERLOOKING A LEARNING DISABILITY?

Step 1: Identify the problem

What are the predominant emotions displayed?

What are the most striking behaviors displayed?

What is the extent of the problem (does it occur elsewhere)?

What is the child's perspective on the problem?

Step 2: Trace the evolution of the problem

When did I (or someone else) first notice the problem?

What else was occurring when the problem began?

When does the problem occur (throughout the day, at specific times, etc.)?

Is it worse on some days or at some times than others?

Step 3: Consider child-related factors, such as stressors, family situation, peer relationships

Consider classroom-related factors, such as the daily schedule, physical environment, and emotional climate of the classroom.

Consider teacher-related factors, including your expectations for your students, what concerns you most about the child, past experiences with these types of problems, and the impact of interventions already attempted.

Step 4: Review the child's academic performance

How is the child's overall performance?

Have there been any recent changes in achievement?

What assignments or tasks seem most difficult?

What are underlying skills that the child needs for these tasks?

Is achievement different in different subjects or content areas?

Step 5: Take steps to intervene

What supports can be offered for the emotional/behavioral problems?

Do the academic difficulties warrant referral to a specialist?

Get consultation about classroom-based interventions for both areas.

MOOD MARKERS—EARLY ELEMENTARY

Write the age-appropriate feeling word onto each symbol; photocopy these onto colored paper and laminate. Place them in a basket or envelope by the classroom door so children can take them as they come into the classroom.

sad/upset

excited/antsy

mad/angry

hurt

scared/worried

happy/cheerful

MOOD MARKERS—LATE ELEMENTARY

gloomy dark cloud
sad/depressed/moody

bright shining star
excited/energetic

flash of lightning
mad/angry/irritable

band-aid
sensitive/touchy

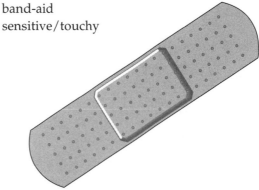

shaking leaf
scared/worried

rays of sunshine
happy/cheerful/hopeful

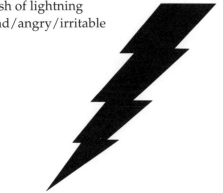
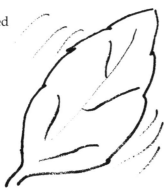

MY PERSONAL PROJECT

My Personal Project is:

These are things I will do to try to achieve my Personal Project:

This is how I will keep track of how I am doing on my Personal Project:

On the days I succeed at my Personal Project, this is how I will reward myself:

On the days I don't succeed, this is how I will get back on track:

5
LEARNING DISABILITIES CAN EXACERBATE EXISTING EMOTIONAL CONDITIONS

When you neglect these language expression problems, these are the kids who get put on Prozac in the eleventh grade.

—Mel Levine, MD
Pediatrician specializing
in learning differences
(Colvin, 1999)

A learning disability is expected to affect academic achievement. What is less frequently noticed, however, is how a learning disability can also affect coexisting emotional problems. This is different from the emotional and psychological consequences of having a learning disability. Rather, specific learning deficits can perpetuate or actually worsen the child's already existing emotional condition. Receiving remedial services can lessen the impact of a learning disability on achievement, but academic intervention may not be completely successful in addressing the emotional issues. Having an understanding of how cognitive deficits affect emotional functioning can be helpful for implementing appropriate interventions.

One main way in which cognitive deficits affect children's emotional functioning is in how they interpret themselves and their social environment (Bender & Wall, 1994). This is most obvious in cases of depression. Depression is not only an affective (emotional) state when a person feels sad and hopeless and has a lack of energy. It is also a cognitive state, with patterns of thinking that perpetuate the depression. For example, 8-year-old Raoul's feelings of hopelessness were fueled by thoughts such as "No one likes me" and "I'll never have any friends." Executive functioning deficits can also affect a child's interpretation of themselves. For instance, problems in reasoning and drawing conclusions can lead children to erroneously believe they are being rejected. They may withdraw as a result, which only worsens their isolation. Children may also apply faulty reasoning to themselves and conclude they are "stupid." Consequently, they give up trying to do well and receive failing grades, which confirms their view and deepens their depression. Such a pessimistic mind-set requires specific intervention, such as cognitive restructuring. Essentially, this entails replacing negative thoughts with more realistic positive ones. Getting a child to stop thinking and saying "I'm so dumb" or "I can't do this" decreases pessimism and the possibility of a self-fulfilling prophecy. Although it sounds simplistic, if done consistently over time, this type of cognitive restructuring is very effective at reducing depression.

Cognitive deficits can also lead children to make attributions that are self-defeating, such as attributing their successes to luck or teacher impulse rather than to their efforts or ability. Believing that they are not in control of their performance (and consequently, their status among peers or acceptance by the teacher) may further result in feelings of anxiety and depression. A closer look at how specific deficits can burden emotional functioning may make it easier to understand how learning disabilities can exacerbate emotional problems. Remember that a child with deficits in one area is likely to have related deficits. For example, a child with a primary attention deficit will also have problems with memory. If a child pays only fleeting attention to something, they will have fewer cues to facilitate recall of the information. The case study at the end of the chapter provides a picture of how this interaction may be played out in a child's life.

LANGUAGE

Children's language processing abilities can significantly affect their emotions. Phonological processing, receptive language skills, and expressive language abilities all affect a child's relationships and experiences. Some researchers postulate that the neurological deficit that is responsible for language impairment underlies problems in understanding nonverbal communication, such as the social meaning of gestures and facial expressions, and discriminating among vocal tones (Holder & Kirkpatrick, 1991; Spafford & Grosser, 1993). If children have difficulty processing language because of phonological deficits, they may not hear others correctly. As a result, they can misinterpret what others say to and about them. For example, a child may think he is being called "fat," when in fact it is another student with the name Pat that is being whispered by a peer.

Receptive language deficits may mean a child has problems understanding spoken instructions. This could cause difficulty both inside and outside the classroom. For example, a child's inability to understand the rules of a group game could cause that child to make mistakes that lead to peer rejection. In class, asking for directions repeatedly may lead to teacher exasperation. Children with expressive language difficulties may not be able to convey their thoughts or respond to others as they wish (e.g., they may speak slowly or vaguely). Such struggles can also lead to peer rejection. Isolation at such a young age is likely to negatively affect self-esteem and may increase depression and anxiety.

Reading difficulties may also worsen preexisting externalizing behavior problems (Cornwall & Bawden, 1992). Specifically, failure to complete homework assignments, lack of interest in academics, and overall difficulty in acquiring academic skills may lead to future academic underachievement, which continues the cycle of delinquency. Reading problems may also contribute to a child's negative internal state. For example, a child with dyslexia may have difficulty reading the daily classroom schedule and, as a result, appear perpetually confused. This ongoing frustration may create social problems for children or may make them angry with themselves.

In all these cases, the students' language deficits make their daily interactions more difficult and increase their overall level of stress. It is easy to understand how this taxes children's resources so much so that they have little emotional reserve. Any existing emotional problems are consequently at risk for becoming worse.

LANGUAGE GAMES

Children with language-based learning disabilities may experience a great deal of frustration, not only with academics but also with everyday living. Teachers can reduce the frustration of these students by introducing simple language games that challenge children but also give them plenty of opportunity to experience success. One such game is Silly Sentences, which can be used at all grade levels. The game requires you to keep a Tupperware box or other container filled with individual words printed on colorful index cards or cardstock. Have students take turns choosing two or three words from the box to see if they can make a meaningful sentence using those words. You can keep the game interesting by adding new words (such as weekly vocabulary lists) and by increasing the number of words the students pick out. Using a point system may make the game more interesting for older children; however, be careful not to let the activity become a competition. It is, after all, a game you are playing to try to increase children's pleasure with communication and language. A list of sample words for the Silly Sentences game can be found at the end of this chapter.

Another language game that can be used to bolster language skills is I Spy. This game of silently choosing an object in the classroom and having students guess what it is, given your description, can be modified for different subjects and ability levels. For example, for young children, you can focus your descriptors on size, color, and shape (e.g., "I spy a big green rectangle" when describing the chalkboard). Use objects that all begin or end with the same letter to reinforce letter-sound correspondences (e.g., "I spy something that begins with the *buh* sound and ends with the *duh* sound."). For older children, the descriptions can be made more complicated by focusing on characteristics such as the purpose of the object and size dimensions (e.g., "I spy an object that I use to remind you of assignments and that is three times as long as it is high" for the chalkboard). You can also use objects that all belong to a category (e.g., things you can communicate with) and have students guess the category. In addition to strengthening language skills, this also builds reasoning and concept formation abilities. I Spy can also be adapted for use with specific subject matter, such as mathematics, by using math-specific descriptors (e.g., "I spy an object whose height measures 1 yard and whose length is twice its height" for the chalkboard). Enhance learning by asking students to explain how they got the correct answer so other children can build their internal problem-solving abilities. You can also make I Spy into a student-driven activity by placing premade I Spy sheets for children to use as a quiet center activity with a partner. An example of an I Spy Activity Sheet can be found at the end of this chapter. Again, the purpose is to make language use and oral communication fun for students who may struggle with language disorders.

To focus on a few letter-sound correspondences, consider the language game Phonics Twister. You can create a simple game board by using a plastic table cloth or shower curtain, on which you can draw circles (in permanent ink) equidistant from each other. Using note cards, write words that begin or end with the featured letters and affix them to each circle using double-sided tape. A spinner can be fashioned by placing a paper plate on top of a piece of thick cardboard. Use a thumbtack to secure a Popsicle stick in the middle. Draw lines to divide the spinner into 8 or 10 sections, with each section bearing one letter. An example highlighting the vowel *a* and several consonants can be found on the Phonics Twister at the end of this chapter. One student should be designated as a "judge," who spins for each turn, announces the sound of the letter (not the name of the letter), and decides if players have acted correctly. Each student in the pair or triad playing should try to place a hand or foot on a word that begins or ends with the sound that the judge has spun. Because children enjoy this active game, you may want to use it as a free choice activity, or be prepared to tolerate some giggling.

Phonemic awareness can also be strengthened by activities involving nonsense syllables. For example, you can write the letters of the alphabet onto individual cards (having two complete sets and a few extra vowels is helpful). Have children blindly pick cards (as few as two or as many as six) and try to make nonsense words out of them. Alternatively, you can randomly pick out a few, arrange them, and ask the student to pronounce the "word." To emphasize a particular letter, have students read sets of two similar words (e.g., "plag" and "pleg"). A fun class activity is to string nonsense syllables together to make a silly lengthy word (in the spirit of Mary Poppins's "supercalifragilisticexpialidocious." At the beginning of each day, create your syllable by having a different student choose and arrange a few letters. Add it to the previous day's syllables until your silly word covers the length of the wall (or the room).

ATTENTION, CONCENTRATION, AND MEMORY

Attention and concentration problems can also exacerbate emotional disorders, straining social interactions. Failing to notice crucial details in nonverbal behavior may make it difficult for a child to understand a speaker's intent. Sarcasm is a good example of this. The remark "Of course I won't give you homework today" means very different things when said with a smile as opposed to a smirk and rolling eyes. Lacking focused attention can also cause problems in a child's conversations with peers. For instance, Steven, a third grader, found it very difficult to focus on anything for more than a few minutes. His peers' patience for his frequent changes of topic and inability to follow the conversation were increasingly short-lived. Eventually, they simply ignored Steven's comments. Peers may also become easily frustrated when lessons are repeatedly interrupted to get a distractible child to focus his or her attention or return to the task. Over time, those social problems can worsen isolation, depression, and low self-esteem.

Memory problems are closely related to problems with attention and concentration. Memory is a major component of how we experience the world. What we remember colors our view of ourselves and others. A child with memory problems may have difficulty recalling enough information to have a realistic sense of self. Because of cognitive distortions (faulty thinking) that are common to depression, a child with deficits in memory may be particularly vulnerable to remembering only those things that confirm his or her reasons for depression. For example, 9-year-old Tanya tended only to remember negative comments from peers or corrective remarks from her teacher and to forget instances when she was praised or recognized positively. Similarly, children who are anxious about their performance may become even more scared and worried if they vividly recall failures but not successes. Memory deficits can also interfere by limiting the amount of information children have at their disposal when needing to draw a conclusion. Suggestions for facilitating attention, concentration, and memory can be found in Overcoming Learning Barriers at the end of this chapter.

REASONING AND MAKING INFERENCES

Some research suggests that children with learning disabilities have inadequate reasoning abilities, such as in making social inferences (Bruno, 1981). Deficits in inference, in making assumptions, and in drawing conclusions can also affect a child's emotional state. For example, if a child who is depressed greets a peer and the peer does not respond, the child may feel personally slighted. In fact, the peer may not have heard the child or may have responded nonverbally. The false conclusion "He doesn't like me" is likely to increase the child's sense of isolation and rejection and may compound depression.

Identifying accurate cause-and-effect relationships is also important. A child who does poorly on a writing assignment may conclude that it is because she is "stupid," rather than that the directions were ambiguous. The opposite is also possible. Tommy, an 8-year-old, had such trouble with cause-and-effect relationships that he often could not understand why he was being rewarded or disciplined. This made it difficult to use reinforcement as a major means of controlling his undesirable behavior. Similarly, children who are denied their teacher's attention may believe that they are not well liked by the teacher, rather than seeing that their timing was inappropriate because there was a lesson in progress. Again, failing to identify true cause-and-effect relationships can contribute to additional feelings of depression and helplessness.

It is important, therefore, to make sure that your students understand your reasoning for correcting them, whether the correction pertains to their behavior or their class work. Being as specific as possible is useful in teaching reasoning skills to children. For example, rather than saying, "I gave you a lower grade because your essay was poorly written," you might explain, "You didn't do as well as you normally do, because you were not specific enough on this assignment. You only gave one example, and I said I wanted at least four." If you sense some mistaken beliefs that are affecting the child's emotional condition, address them directly, such as by saying, "A bad grade doesn't mean you are stupid. It means that you can improve that assignment to make it much better." Ideas for ways to build reasoning skills can be found in Overcoming Learning Barriers at the end of this chapter.

SELF-REGULATION AND VERBAL MEDIATION

The concept of self-regulation refers in part to the ability to monitor and adjust oneself to meet the demands of a situation. It is believed that the development of self-regulation begins with significant others controlling the child's behavior through the use of verbal directives and reflections (e.g., "If you climb on that bookcase, you'll fall and hurt yourself"). This speech becomes internalized by children over time, so that they then may think similar thoughts or say similar things to themselves to try to direct their own behavior (Vygotsky, 1978). For example, children who had been chastised by their parents for stealing from the cookie jar may say to themselves, "I'm going to get in trouble if I take a cookie without asking first," which may lead them to restrain themselves (at least temporarily). Self-regulation is needed for both emotions and behavior and for cognition (e.g., problem-solving).

Verbal mediation, a specific aspect of self-regulation, refers to the use of "self-talk" or an internal dialogue as a means of facilitating performance. When problem solving about a strained relationship, for example, you might say to yourself, "Okay, what are my options? I could try to talk to my friend, but it will probably only make me feel angrier, because she doesn't understand. I could write her a letter to explain my actions, and maybe that will help us to talk." Verbal mediation entails identifying possible courses of action and the benefits and drawbacks of each option before taking any action. If you skipped this step, you would act based solely on your feelings or impulses, which would often lead to negative outcomes.

Children with learning disabilities, such as substantial verbal deficits (e.g., reading disabilities), use less task-relevant private speech than normally achieving children (Harris, 1986; Richman & Lindgren, 1981). Not only does this affect their learning, but it also affects their behavior. For example, children with deficits in emotional self-regulation may not naturally use internal speech to guide their behavior. Because they are unable to appropriately reflect on their behavior and to control their arousal level, they may become overstimulated and not be able to calm themselves down. Consequently, they may be more prone to acting out or behaving disruptively. Because of deficits in self-regulation, the same child may not be able to behave appropriately in a situation (e.g., using a quiet voice indoors) or may take longer to adjust to transitions (e.g., going from the classroom to the art room). It is important to understand that it is not that children are not capable of knowing what the correct behavior is, but that they have trouble actually producing the appropriate response (Egan, Brown, Goonan, Goonan, & Celano, 1998). The case study that follows of Mee is an example of how self-regulation problems can exacerbate a child's emotional problems.

There are many ways to encourage the development of both emotional and cognitive self-regulation. Role plays and case discussions can be helpful, because they bring internal dialogue into the open. Giving a scenario and then asking students to think about possible responses and how they would choose among those actions is a simple activity that can be expanded to accommodate any time constraint. Possible scenarios include how to deal with frustration during a writing assignment, what to do if someone teases you, and how to handle a disappointing grade. Allowing children to settle their own disputes can also facilitate the development of self-regulation (Bronson, 2000). Verbal mediation in particular should be reinforced for children with Attention-Deficit/ Hyperactivity Disorder (ADHD), as it provides a crucial middle step between impulse and action. For example, a child with ADHD may be taught to "Stop, Think and Act," and to remind themselves of this each time they have to decide what to do. A Stop, Think, Act reproducible bearing these reminders can be found at the end of this chapter.

Self-instructional techniques, such as those developed by Meichenbaum (1984), can facilitate the development of cognitive self-regulation. The five steps to his self-instructional techniques include (1) defining the problem ("What do I have to do?"), (2) planning and response guidance ("What materials do I need?"), (3) self-reinforcement ("I know how to do this"), (4) self-evaluation ("Have I done all the parts?"), and (5) coping ("I need some help"). These cues are provided in poster format at the end of this chapter on the Self-Instruction reproducible and should be referred to at the start of assignments that require independent functioning. When your students approach you for help, lead them through the questions so they gradually become used to doing it on their own.

✧ CASE STUDY: The Overwhelmed Child

Mee, aged 9, came from a large family. As the oldest child, she was expected to be a "good example" and help with child care for her other five siblings. By nature a serious child, Mee took her responsibilities very seriously. Although she often felt burdened and overwhelmed, she still tried to meet all of her parents' and teachers' expectations.

Unfortunately, Mee had serious learning problems, which included problems with self-regulation. This meant that she often acted before she had thought through the consequences of her actions. She frequently interrupted others, such as answering a question even before it had been completed. She often seemed unprepared, because she failed to consider what she needed to do to accomplish the task. In addition, she had trouble organizing herself, requiring much direction from her teacher. Her teacher once remarked, "I have to tell Mee to get out or put away her books and pencils so many times a day that I feel like a broken record." Since Mee did not naturally use self-talk to guide her behavior, she had a hard time implementing the study and writing process strategies her teacher taught, because these required asking herself questions such as "What is the central idea?" This was frustrating for both Mee and her teacher, because it made her less independent than the other students.

These learning problems not only made school difficult, but Mee also felt the burden of them on her home life and emotional well-being. Her parents constantly criticized her for interrupting, which they perceived as not having proper manners, and for being disrespectful to her teacher by not being prepared for lessons. They were ashamed of her failings and often accused her of "not caring" about how her behavior was affecting the family's reputation. Mee often replied though tears, "I'm trying!" Mee seemed to become more disappointed and frustrated in herself as the year wore on. Though her parents would not even consider it, her teacher wondered whether she should refer Mee for counseling for depression.

METACOGNITIVE ABILITIES

Being able to take a step back and reflect on oneself, particularly one's cognitive processes and thinking, is an important metacognitive ability. This is different from self-regulation and verbal mediation, because it focuses on "thinking about thinking" rather than thinking about what to do. Metacognitive skills include knowing what techniques are needed to accomplish a task and monitoring one's use of those strategies (Baker & Brown, 1984).

Children whose metacognitive skills are weak are less aware of their strengths and weaknesses and have fewer resources to learn adaptive and compensatory skills. For example, if children are unable to recognize that organizing symbols is difficult for them, they may struggle unsuccessfully to write neatly, rather than using a ruler to guide their writing. Being aware of personal difficulties facilitates help-seeking behaviors. If children were able to look at an assignment and think to themselves, "I'm going to have to do a lot of reading to do this assignment, and reading is hard for me," they might be able to access the teacher's assistance or use previously learned compensatory strategies (such as breaking the task into smaller units) before beginning the task, rather than when they have become thoroughly disappointed and fatigued. For many children with learning disabilities, however, awareness of their specific learning problems does not occur until after they have already experienced a great deal of frustration and failure. Failure to develop this type of metacognition may consequently worsen already existing depression and low self-esteem.

Metacognition also is important in problem solving. The child whose metacognitive abilities are limited may also struggle with problem solving, which may contribute to feelings of helplessness and hopelessness. Rather than being able to isolate areas of cognitive weakness, children may feel that they "can't do anything right." Such helplessness can lead to greater apathy, as well as feeling depressed and giving up. Deficits in metacognition can also increase anxiety, since the child cannot ward off feelings of panic or dread by proactively enlisting helping strategies. This is true in the case of Tanika, a 10-year-old whose learning disability led to anxiety and avoidance. Tanika would begin to feel anxious when confronted with a potentially difficult assignment, and she would not start supportive actions, such as getting out her learning aids or asking for clarification, until she was so worked up that the teacher had to intervene.

SOCIAL ADJUSTMENT

Students with learning disabilities who are integrated into the regular classroom are more often rejected or isolated than their nondisabled peers (Fox, 1989; Roberts & Zubrick, 1993). Some believe that students with learning disabilities display more aggression and misconduct in the classroom (see the literature review by Cornwall & Bawden, 1992), leading to their rejection. Others believe that the actual incidence of disruptive behavior is not higher, but that regular education students judge the disruptive behavior of the students with disabilities more harshly (Roberts & Zubrick, 1993). The possibility that students with learning disabilities are judged differently than nondisabled students was also evident in Juvonen and Bear's (1992) study. The researchers found that girls with learning disabilities held the most negative social status in the integrated classroom, perhaps because of their perceived deviance from the stereotypical norm of academic and social competence.

Another possibility is that students with learning disabilities demonstrate less social competence than their nondisabled peers (Hiebert, Wong, & Hunter, 1982; Sabornie, 1994). Some evidence suggests that students with learning disabilities have difficulty decoding subtle nonverbal social cues such as facial expressions (LaGreca, 1981). For example, children with learning disabilities require more time to interpret emotions than children without learning disabilities and may have trouble interpreting specific emotions such as surprise and disgust (Holder & Kirkpatrick, 1991). You can imagine how misinterpreting disgust as surprise could lead to rejection. Ineffective social behavior can also compound existing peer relationship problems. Children who lack basic skills such as initiating a conversation, taking turns, and providing positive feedback to others may experience many negative social interactions. Unfortunately, children with learning disabilities also tend to use fewer coping and problem-solving strategies in social situations (Parril-Burnstein, 1981), which only worsens existing social problems. For example, children whose language problems make friendships difficult may also have a hard time figuring out ways to strengthen their relationships. Not being able to adjust, negotiate, or creatively resolve social disputes may create additional confusion and sadness. Resentment can build if the child feels misunderstood or is repeatedly rejected. Because peer relationships become increasingly important as children mature, such experiences can affect children's view of themselves and their self-esteem. Children who see themselves as unable to make friends or rejected by peers, in addition to having academic problems, may feel even more inferior or fundamentally flawed.

Beyond deficits in specific social skills, children with learning disabilities are also thought to have less interpersonal understanding than nondisabled peers. Specifically, children with learning disabilities tend to be more egocentric and consequently are less affected by others' points of view (Kravetz, Faust, Lipshitz, & Shalhav, 1999). As a result, such children may not understand why others are rejecting them or judging them to be disobedient, when in fact, they were merely wrapped up in their own worlds. In part, this may be due to a difficulty in taking another's perspective or may be related to problems with social inferences. This apparent obliviousness can worsen already strained peer relationships.

Opinions differ on where to intervene, though the most successful interventions will depend on a variety of child, classroom, and teacher factors. For example, children with learning disabilities may lack social competence because of insufficient experiences. You can help by providing specific social feedback to your students with learning disabilities. For example, you may want to specifically praise instances in which children used effective social skills or help them understand why a particular social interaction was unsuccessful. Ideally, these interventions would be used with your entire class, since whole classroom strategies based on cooperation and mutual assistance have been found to promote friendship (Janney & Snell, 1996). See Developing Social Skills at the end of this chapter for additional ideas. For maximum impact, teach social skills in situations that are naturally occurring, such as when students complains that others are teasing them. To reinforce concepts, you can also use role plays or discuss scenarios with the entire class.

Alternatively, you may decide to take a less global approach and focus on one particular aspect of social skills. For example, in studies of social competence among students with learning disabilities, "children with learning disabilities perceived themselves as being socially accepted because they had at least one friend in their class" (Juvonen & Bear, 1992, p. 327). Rather than attempting to instruct a student on all areas of social functioning, it may be more reasonable to concentrate on nurturing a specific friendship for a child with learning disabilities. Pairing a nondisabled student with a student with learning disabilities on the basis of mutual interests has also been found to be effective for promoting positive peer relationships (Fox, 1989). Without adult intervention, students without disabilities tend to interact more with nondisabled peers rather than those with disabilities (Sale & Carey, 1995). Consequently, it is "imperative that teachers perform some type of intervention in order for mainstreamed (LD) children to successfully be integrated socially into the regular classroom. Otherwise, teachers may anticipate a drop in children's acceptance as the year progresses" (Fox, 1989, p. 57).

RELATED INTERACTIONS

In addition to characteristics of the learning disability affecting the child's emotional functioning, aspects associated with having a learning disability may also further exacerbate preexisting emotional disturbance. For example, some children feel isolated or stigmatized by having to leave the classroom for remedial services. Although pull-out services may be necessary and effective, they necessarily cause children to miss out on the experiences of their classroom peers, mundane as those may be. Consistently missing the same classroom activity can result in children feeling left out and not as integrated into the classroom as their peers. In addition, being the only child with an identified learning disability, similar to being the only child of a particular ethnic group, may make the student feel particularly isolated and different (Juvonen & Bear, 1992).

Furthermore, the views of others toward children with learning disabilities may result in additional shame, anger, or defensiveness. Well-meaning teachers and support personnel may talk down to children with learning disabilities or assume that they cannot do the same activity as their peers because of their deficits. Drawing such negative attention to children's deficits may influence the views of their peers, which may in turn result in further isolation or rejection. Teasing is a natural part of childhood. Having an identified difference, such as a learning disability, can unfortunately provide a consistent target for teasing and mockery by peers.

Some of the examples provided in this chapter illustrate how the nature of the cognitive deficits negatively affects emotional functioning. Others were situations in which the learning disability interacted with the child's social functioning, which in turn affected the child's emotional well-being and self-concept. This external feedback loop is obvious. In addition, in older children in particular, the internal self-evaluative processes can have even more impact than the reactions of others. Children who are sensitive, perfectionistic, timid, or have low self-esteem may be only minimally influenced by others. Instead, they may be their own worst enemies, judging their performance (both academic and interpersonal) more harshly than others. Thus, it is not necessarily just the environment that interacts with the learning disability to produce negative emotional states. It may be well within the child and their constitution to react in such a manner.

For example, helping children express their feelings appropriately is a basic intervention for both internalizing and externalizing disorders. However, for many children with language-based learning disabilities, emphasizing "talking it out" may be more frustrating than helpful. Finding other means of emotional release, such as through drawing, music, exercise, or physical activity, may be more effective coping for these children. It is also possible that interventions themselves further intensify emotional problems. It is important to find creative ways to heal children's emotional problems that do not depend on skills central to their learning disabilities.

✦ CASE STUDY: The Isolated Child

Jenna had been held back in first grade for being a "slow learner," so that now, at age 12, she was a sixth grader. She was recently diagnosed as having a Mixed Receptive-Expressive Language Disorder, only after it became quite obvious that Jenna did not simply need more time or maturity to catch up to her peers. In fact, Jenna's significant phonological deficits had so affected her reading and writing that she was almost two grade levels behind her classmates (and almost three levels from her age peers), though she was at grade level in math.

In addition to her academic problems, however, Jenna had some significant emotional and psychological problems. Ever since she entered school, Jenna had been very quiet and shy. Now she was withdrawn, almost to the point of being isolated. Since she didn't have any real friends, Jenna hid herself in music. Any time she could, she had her earphones on, listening to her Walkman. Jenna also seemed very uneasy, not just in academic and group social settings but even in one-to-one situations. Her counselor noted how she had trouble having a conversation with him—Jenna tended not to maintain eye contact and had nervous habits like biting her nails and shifting anxiously from foot to foot. In addition, because early on Jenna's inconsistent academic performance had been explained as her being "unmotivated," "slow to learn," or even "lazy" for many years, Jenna seemed to have developed a poor sense of self. She was easily discouraged by her continued difficulties and seemed increasingly depressed.

Concern for Jenna's poor achievement and social adjustment led her teachers, parents, and school-based support team to gather to talk about options for school the following year. Her academic skills were insufficient for a junior high curriculum, but Jenna was resistant to the idea of having special help in junior high because she thought it would make her "seem like a freak" to her peers. Her parents did not want to impose such help, for fear that it would lead her to hate school. However, since she had already been held back once, repeating sixth grade did not seem to be a good option.

During the course of that discussion, it became apparent that not only had Jenna's learning disability contributed significantly to her anxiety and depression, but it was also worsening it. Her reading problems and problems interpreting what others said seemed to make Jenna perpetually disoriented in the classroom, which only heightened her anxiety. She was constantly distracted by her worries, which compounded the memory deficits associated with her language problems. Unfortunately, not being able to remember things contributed to both her learning problems and her self-image, which centered around the fact that she was "dumb."

Jenna's desire to fade into the backdrop also led her to refuse remedial help and interventions. For example, she was ashamed of her problem spelling even basic words and disliked using her spell checker. If she had to concentrate intensely for a period, such as during reading lessons, she would tire out, leaving her too fatigued to do well in the next activity. As a result, she sometimes seemed zoned out and often had to be reminded to pay attention. She hated being singled out like that and seemed to sulk for a while afterward.

Jenna's social isolation was making itself worse—the more she withdrew, the less her peers wanted to spend time with her. In addition, they quickly tired of repeating themselves when she misunderstood. Many had given up trying to talk with her. This made her feel even worse about herself. Her poor self-image often got in the way of her overcoming her disability, since she tended to give up, feeling hopeless that she could do any better.

MINIMIZING THE EFFECTS OF COGNITIVE DEFICITS

In addition to the academic accommodations and remedial help provided for your students with learning disabilities, consider addressing the related cognitive deficits as well so they are less likely to spill over into other areas of functioning. You can find suggestions for ways to address problems in memory, self-regulation, and other cognitive skills in Overcoming Learning Barriers, found at the end of this chapter.

It is also helpful to discuss the ways in which learning disabilities affect emotional functioning with your students, particularly if they are older and more able to independently monitor themselves. Building their awareness of the role their cognitive deficits play in their social interactions is useful, because it provides them with the ability to avoid such problems. For example, if children with nonverbal learning disabilities understand how their spatial problems are making their social isolation worse, they may be more motivated to improve their skills or may be more careful not to let them get in the way.

SUMMARY

Specific cognitive deficits, such as language, attention, memory, and reasoning problems, can exacerbate emotional problems by affecting how children interpret their environment and think about themselves. In addition, self-regulation problems and social skills deficits strain social interactions and may make it more difficult to exhibit appropriate classroom behavior. Problems in meta-cognitive abilities can also decrease a child's internal resources for coping. Classroom interventions include specific activities to build deficit areas, such as teaching the use of verbal mediation. It is also helpful to make your students aware of the impact their learning disability can have on their interpersonal relationships and emotional health.

SILLY SENTENCES

Photocopy and enlarge this list, laminate it, cut out the words, and store them in a box.

accident	bottle	enemy	hold	neighbor	secret
adult	boy	escape	homework	never	sick
afraid	brag	emergency	honest	nice	silly
allowance	brave	face	house	note	sister
alone	brother	fall	illness	old	smart
anger	bug	famous	invisible	orange	snake
annoy	cake	father	jealous	ostrich	soap
ant	camera	fear	joke	owl	song
ape	candy	feeling	kangaroo	owner	sorry
apple	car	fire engine	kind	paint	sticker
ashamed	catch	first	lady	party	strong
automobile	cheat	fix	large	pay	talk
baby	chew	flower	last	picnic	teacher
baby-sitter	children	forget	late	play	tease
bad	clean	fox	learn	pretty	teenager
bad luck	clothing	friend	leave	prince	telephone
balloon	copy	garbage	lion	prize	test
bath	counselor	gift	lonely	problem	thought
beat	cowboy	girl	love	proud	tickle
beautiful	danger	grade	magic	queen	under
beaver	desk	grown-up	market	question	umbrella
behavior	dinosaur	gum	manners	quiet	velvet
belong	directions	hamster	mean	report	vest
belly button	dirt	hand	message	reward	whisper
best	disgust	happy	miracle	robber	wish
bicycle	doll	hat	mirror	sad	wonder
birthday	dream	help	mistake	scary	young
black	egg	hide	mother	school	zoo

I SPY ACTIVITY SHEET

I SPY

Name _____

Partner's name _____

I spy a . . .

(size) _____

(shape) _____

(color) _____

(other description) _____

that you can use to _____

_____.

My partner's guesses are: Correct?

1) _____   Yes   No

2) _____   Yes   No

3) _____   Yes   No

The correct answer is _____.

ACTIVITY: PHONICS TWISTER

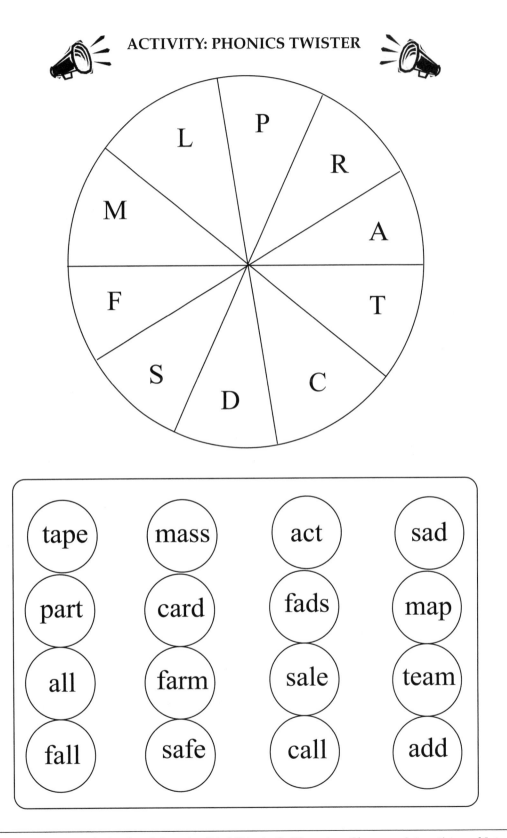

STOP, THINK, ACT

 # STOP
Take a deep breath.

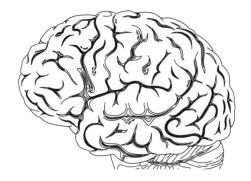 # THINK
What are my options?

 # ACT
Act, then reevaluate.

SELF-INSTRUCTION

DEFINE THE PROBLEM

What do I have to do?

PLAN

How am I going to do this?

What materials do I need?

REINFORCE YOURSELF

I have confidence in myself!

I can do it!

EVALUATE

Have I done all the parts?

What else do I need to do?

COPE

Do I need to take a break?

Should I get some help?

DEVELOPING SOCIAL SKILLS

AWARENESS OF SELF IN RELATION TO OTHERS

♦ Spatial sense—Am I too close? too far?

♦ Voice volume—Is it the same as other people?

♦ Activity level—Am I the only one moving around?

♦ Reading others' reactions—How are other people responding to me?

COMMUNICATION

♦ Using "I statements"—Say how you feel, not how the other person made you feel.

♦ Listening—Eyes on the speaker, wait until they stop speaking for your turn.

♦ Asking questions—Address the person by name and be specific.

CONFLICT RESOLUTION

♦ Dealing with teasing—If it's true, what can you do about it? If not, ignore it.

♦ Apologizing—Say what you are sorry for, and make sure the other person believes you.

♦ Taking responsibility—If you made a mistake, admit it. Do something to fix it.

COOPERATION

♦ Compromising—Each person gives in a little to get a little.

♦ Taking turns—After you have talked or done something once, wait and see if anyone else wants to.

♦ Expressing appreciation—Compliment people for their talents, and thank them for help.

ASSERTIVENESS

♦ Making a request—Figure out exactly what you want, be polite, and ask, don't demand.

♦ Advocating for yourself—Don't hide your problems; ask for what you need.

OVERCOMING LEARNING BARRIERS

ATTENTION AND CONCENTRATION

- ♦ Have the student sit closest to the part of the room where you teach the most (not necessarily by the blackboard or by your desk).

- ♦ Try giving children a paper clip to keep in their pocket that they can fiddle with when they feel like getting out of their seat.

- ♦ Provide ear plugs for use during testing.

- ♦ Make one request at a time. Wait until it is completed before giving the next direction.

- ♦ Provide visual cues when giving directions.

- ♦ Allow for frequent short breaks to stretch or walk around during long lessons.

- ♦ Vary your tone of voice, volume, and rate of speech. Whispering can be very attention-grabbing.

MEMORY

- ♦ Teach the use of mnemonics, such as making up a song with the information to be memorized, creating a sentence with the first letter of each word, or pairing visual images with words.

- ♦ Encourage the use of a small notebook, especially for recording home-work assignments.

- ♦ Teach the student how to use a day planner to note tests, due dates, and other requirements.

- ♦ Use repetition when giving directions, and have students repeat them back to you.

- ♦ Give both written and verbal reminders.

- ♦ For frequently used directions, have a cue card with the directions already written on it to place in front of the class.

REASONING

- ♦ Make up scenarios to discuss cause-and-effect relationships.

- ♦ Ask students why common things happen (e.g., "Why do we line up for lunch?").

- ♦ Explain your rationale for rewards, corrections, and discipline.

- ♦ Create "what if" questions for discussion (e.g., "What if we didn't have school?").

SELF-REGULATION

- ♦ Encourage students to take breaks as needed to refresh themselves for the task.

- ♦ Teach relaxation techniques, such as deep breathing, for use prior to tests or difficult assignments.

- ♦ Encourage appropriate accessing of help and support from others.

- ♦ Help students develop short-term goals for long assignments.

- ♦ Remind students to "Stop, Think, and Act" and emphasize the evaluation process after an action has been taken.

6
EMOTIONAL PROBLEMS CAN INTENSIFY LEARNING DISORDERS

There is very little access to the brain when the heart is in pain.

—Janet E. Hart, MEd
Fourth-grade teacher
4 years of teaching experience
West Yarmouth, Massachusetts

Although learning disabilities and cognitive deficits can exacerbate emotional problems, the reverse is also possible. Whether emotional problems are a consequence of the learning disorder or coexist due to other life stressors, they can intensify learning problems. Emotional problems may directly affect a child's learning disability by compounding the initial cognitive deficits. Alternatively, they may indirectly influence achievement by reducing the resources children have to overcome their learning disabilities.

AVOIDANCE AND PASSIVITY

One major way cognitive deficits can be made worse is when the child's coping methods interfere with learning. Emotional problems such as anxiety and hopelessness can lead a child to avoid upsetting tasks and to shy away from challenging material. Unfortunately, this initial behavior can lead to a cycle of avoidance that is hard to break. Specifically, children learn over time that avoiding difficult situations lessens their anxiety. This reinforcement only produces additional incentive to avoid challenging situations in the future. Eventually, the child becomes so accustomed to avoiding that it becomes a primary method of coping. This results in a belief that the problem is insurmountable, which decreases the child's self-confidence and desire to take risks to meet a challenge. In addition, children are likely to fall further and further behind in their academic achievement due to failure to acquire additional skills. Remediation becomes more difficult because there are fewer foundational skills on which to rely.

This cycle of avoidance stood in the way of 10-year-old André's improving his oral reading ability. André learned that if he was called on to read, he could pretend to "stumble" over a word and take a long time reading the first sentence. This was often good enough to get the teacher to call on someone else. Because he used this technique to avoid having to read aloud, André's oral reading became even more dysfluent.

You can help children who rely on avoidance by not "rescuing" them and instead providing the minimum amount of guidance necessary. For example, to deal with André's reading fears, it would be helpful to continue to call on André to read aloud and to agree to take turns reading (e.g., he reads one sentence, then you read one, until the passage is done), rather than to excuse him from reading aloud or purposely choose brief passages for him to read. You can gradually fade your guidance (e.g., he reads two sentences, you read one). This conveys the message that approaching a problem with assistance is better than running away from it.

In addition to anxiety, passivity can also interfere with learning. Having to constantly deal with one's learning disabilities can be overwhelming and tiring, thereby reducing children's tolerance for their disability and motivation to overcome it. This attitude is akin to thinking, "What's the use; I can't do anything about it anyway." Passivity may prevent the child from exploring creative compensatory methods or from accessing support and assistance (Halmhuber & Paris, 1993). Consequently, although children may be capable of implementing alternative learning strategies, they are less likely to do so. In addition, children's goals may change from overcoming their disabilities to merely "passing" or "getting through school," which also reduces the chances that they will be active and creative in their struggle with learning (Barga, 1996).

Suggestions for building healthier coping skills, especially in older elementary students, can be found in the Building Coping Skills section at the end of this chapter. Discuss them with your students, then post them around the classroom in places they are likely to see them often (e.g., where they wait in line). The more you reinforce the use of those skills, the more natural they will become to your students. This familiarity and ease will enable them to use the methods independently. When they have become natural to your students, you will be able to refer to them simply by using the key words (in boldface) to remind your students of the coping methods.

EXTERNAL LOCUS OF CONTROL

Children with learning disabilities tend to have an external locus of control, meaning that they attribute their successes to something outside themselves, such as luck or teacher whimsy, rather than to something internal, such as effort (Halmhuber & Paris, 1993; Rogers & Saklofske, 1985). At the same time, these children may attribute their failures to stable internal factors, such as ability, which are also beyond their control (Tollefson et al., 1982). This tendency may be due to their lack of understanding about the nature of their disabilities or confusion regarding school tasks and expectations (Halmhuber & Paris, 1993). For example, Margaret, aged 8, did not comprehend that her nonverbal learning disability affected multiple areas of learning. As a result, she repeatedly concluded that her "whole brain was broken" and that she could not do anything about it. She believed that her teachers were mean to challenge her, since "they should know I can't do what other kids can."

Students with learning disabilities who do not feel able to control their academic achievement consequently act as if they are not. The resulting behaviors may even intensify initial learning problems. "When students feel they have little control over their own success and failure in the classroom, they may choose low-risk tasks, invest minimal effort, and give up prematurely when encountering difficulties" (Halmhuber & Paris, 1993, p. 94). If students with learning disabilities are not persistent in their efforts to succeed despite difficulty, it is unlikely that they will learn to overcome their handicaps.

MIND-SET FOR LEARNING

Even if a child's emotional problems are unrelated to his or her learning problems (e.g., if the depression is due to parental divorce), they can spill over into his or her academic performance and functioning. Prior to arriving at school, a student experiences a variety of interactions that can create a mind-set that is not conducive to learning. Children who are fearful of being attacked or hurt in their crime-ridden neighborhood, students who are repeatedly berated by their parent before being put on the school bus, and children who have had to get themselves ready for school because their intoxicated parents could not help are all in a state of emotional crisis. It is unlikely that they will be able to immediately forget their problems once they reach school and invest themselves in learning. More likely, their emotional concerns will continue to distract them throughout the school day. In contrast to normally achieving children, those who have learning disabilities may also begin with more limited cognitive resources from which to draw. What energy they could have used to overcome their learning difficulties in the classroom has been drained by their need to cope with significant emotional issues outside the classroom.

Although you cannot control what a child encounters prior to entering your classroom, there are many ways you can facilitate a positive mind-set for learning. Chapter 7 discusses interventions such as creating a classroom climate conducive to learning and inducing a positive mood. In addition, you can encourage your students to develop personal exercises to help clear their minds. Depending on your students, these may take the form of quiet meditation, deep breathing, a silent prayer, a motivational song, or a personal pep talk—whatever works best for them.

SELF-ESTEEM

Poor self-esteem and self-concept can also negatively affect achievement. Among children with learning disabilities, those who have low self-esteem perform worse academically than those with adequate self-esteem (Kloomok & Cosden, 1994). One explanation for this is that self-concept has a stronger impact than children's overall intellectual ability on their response to remedial efforts (Kershner, 1990). Specifically, "children with auditory-linguistic LD who possess a positive self-image are most likely to benefit from remediation" (Kershner, 1990, p. 372). In addition, having a high self-concept in nonacademic areas may serve as a buffer for academic problems, even among children with learning disabilities, whereas having a poor global self-concept, or inadequacy in both academic and nonacademic arenas, can hinder achievement.

Poor self-esteem and self-concept might also affect achievement by way of a self-fulfilling prophecy. For example, children with low self-esteem may encounter difficulty on a math assignment due to their nonverbal learning disability. The ensuing failure further decreases the students' opinion of themselves. This causes them to put forth less effort on the next assignment and to use fewer creative compensatory strategies. These choices not only result in achievement beneath the children's capability, but it also hinders future academic development, thereby exacerbating their fundamental learning problems.

One of the easiest but most important interventions is to praise students for their hard work, persistence, and effort and to avoid praising them for their ability. Children praised for their intelligence tend to be more concerned with their performance than learning, resulting in their tendency to give up earlier when faced with difficulty. To these children, challenges are seen as threats. "Rewarding children's efforts puts the focus on the process of learning. With this focus, students are less likely to compare their performance to that of others, and are more likely to concentrate on their own performance goals" (Rothbart & Jones, 1998).

DEPRESSION

In addition to its emotional aspects, slowness in responding, difficulty in concentrating, and being easily fatigued are all possible manifestations of depression (Wright-Strawderman & Watson, 1992). These depressive symptoms may emphasize existing cognitive difficulty and lower academic performance for a child who already has processing difficulties.

Depressed children who have learning disabilities have also been found to experience decreases in their academic self-perceptions (Heath, 1995), which may further hamper achievement and academic risk taking. Some believe that this occurs as a function of "negative cognitive distortion," or a tendency to view things in a negative light or to remember only negative information (Lauer et al., 1994). For example, depressed children with learning disabilities may not focus on their achievements or reinforce themselves for what they are doing right. Others argue that depressed children with learning disabilities are actually accurate in their negative perceptions, rather than overdramatizing them (Heath, 1995). Unfortunately, this tendency replaces the coping strategy of "positive distortion" (e.g., children telling themselves or herself that despite their failing grade, they are okay). As a result, children may become increasingly hopeless about their learning potential and lack motivation to acquire compensatory or additional skills as a result.

In a similar vein, several researchers have noted that depression may lead to cognitive errors, such as overgeneralization or selective abstraction (drawing a conclusion without using all the available information) (Leitenberg, Yost, & Carroll-Wilson, 1986). For example, depressed children may overgeneralize from their poor spelling test and feel that they "can't do anything right." They may also selectively ignore contradictory information. In addition, severely depressed children may experience memory impairment, perhaps because they fail to use memory strategies (Lauer et al., 1994). Of particular importance, depressed children do not recall the content of positive events (e.g., a question they answered correctly) as well as children who are not depressed (Whitman & Leitenberg, 1990). Specifically, depressed children have greater difficulty remembering the right answers given to them following their errors. Certainly, poor memory can hinder remedial efforts and interact negatively with preexisting cognitive deficits. As a result, more serious learning problems or greater academic decline may occur. For example, depressed children with learning disabilities may not recall the strategies they previously used to answer a problem correctly. Consequently, they cannot systematically apply that skill or method to another problem. They may also forget teacher feedback about how to answer questions correctly or forget the correct content provided by the teacher. Thus, depression can create learning problems as well as make existing ones worse, such as for Tami, described in the case study that follows.

Lauer and colleagues (1994) suggest two related intervention strategies when dealing with the effects of childhood depression on memory: frequent review and assistance in organizing information for more accurate storage and retrieval. For example, if you are teaching state capitals, you can give multiple examples of how to organize them, such as by geographic region (e.g., New England, West Coast, etc.), alphabetically, or by color on the map. Help your students find the organizational strategy that is easiest for them. Provide frequent review using the most popular methods chosen. These actions will not only strengthen their ability to remember state capitals but will reinforce learning concepts that can be applied independently. Other memory aids, such as those discussed at the end of Chapter 5, may also be helpful for children with depression.

ANXIETY

Anxiety and achievement have been found to have a complex curvilinear relationship where optimal performance is associated with a moderate degree of anxiety and arousal (Sharma, 1970). Extremes of anxiety (none or too much) tend to decrease performance. In school, some "anxiety," or emotional investment in doing well, is necessary for exerting effort, persisting with difficult tasks, and trying to understand and recall information. However, too much anxiety can hamper children's efforts to learn by immobilizing them, causing confusion and disorganization, and interfering with memory. This results in yet another barrier to learning that children with learning disabilities must overcome to succeed.

There is some suggestion that anxious children are particularly attuned to possible impending threat (Taghavi, Neshat-Doost, Moradi, Yule, & Dalgleish, 1999). Consequently, anxious children may be hypervigilant or particularly sensitive to situations that are challenging or threatening. For students with learning disabilities, this may mean that they are very aware of possible situations in which they may fail or be ridiculed. Children with learning disabilities have been found to react more strongly to failure than their nondisabled peers and to have greater difficulty recovering from the anxiety and stress produced (Dean & Rattan, 1987). As a result, these children may be even less equipped to tackle challenging tasks. For example, an anxious student with learning disabilities may not know how to do the third question on a worksheet. The anxiety that results may further decrease that student's problem-solving ability for the fourth question and each question after that. Anxiety seems to subtly affect the problem-solving abilities of children with learning disabilities, perhaps causing them to become less systematic and logical as anxiety increases (Fisher, Allen, & Kose, 1996). Tami, featured in the case study that follows, experienced a high level of anxiety that reduced her ability to meet academic challenges.

You can help anxious children by providing just enough support so that the child is empowered to act. This may mean patiently talking a child through a difficult task, rather than immediately offering help. Acknowledging the child's fears and providing reality-based assurance is also important. For example, if children are anxious about doing poorly on an upcoming test, it is helpful to remind them of their previous successful performance and emphasize things under their control (such as their time studying or their effort) that can influence their performance.

Using relaxation exercises and imagery with anxious children, particularly before they begin hard tasks, is helpful. An example of guided imagery would be to help anxious children let go of their worries so they can begin their work. Tell your students to imagine a peaceful place, such as a forest stream, and to watch their worries float away down the stream (e.g., one worry per fallen leaf). While they are working, if they begin to feel anxious, they can close their eyes, take a deep breath, and imagine the worry floating away, with each exhalation helping it along. Children who are less likely to be familiar with relaxing nature images may prefer something like watching their worries speed out of sight while attached to a subway car. Solicit other images from your students and share them with your class so they will have multiple images from which to choose. This type of guided imagery can be quick and become second nature when practiced often, even for very young children.

Tami had recently moved to the area and entered her third-grade class almost 2 months after school had already begun. With her innocent eyes and delicate features, she looked like a frightened little doe lost in the woods. In fact, Tami was, in a sense, "lost." Upon his release from jail, her father had moved her and her two younger siblings in order to escape a physically abusive mother whose drug abuse had resulted in significant neglect. Because of Tami's chaotic background, her teachers and other school personnel tried to be sensitive to her emotional needs. Not wanting to pressure her, her teacher gave her additional time to adjust to her new environment. Although Tami was behind in her schoolwork, everyone hoped that after a few weeks, she would be comfortable enough to participate fully in class activities.

After winter break, however, Tami still seemed overwhelmed, and she was hopelessly behind in her class work. In particular, her teacher noticed that assignments requiring writing, such as spelling homework, were full of errors and exceptionally sloppy. When Tami's old school records were finally obtained, the teacher noted that reading and writing problems had been present ever since she started school, though initially they seemed mild. A thorough psychoeducational evaluation confirmed that Tami had a significant learning disability in reading and writing. In addition, Tami had signs of clinical depression and a generalized anxiety disorder.

Several factors contributed to the exacerbation of Tami's learning problems. First, despite her unpredictable mother, Tami had had some sense of stability and safety in her previous home because of a caring neighbor who would intervene on behalf of Tami and her siblings. Now that she was in a completely new environment, she did not know where to turn for support. Her father, with whom she had had minimal contact for 2 years, was overwhelmed with making enough money to support his family of four and had little time to attend to her emotional needs. On a daily basis, Tami felt incredibly alone and insecure. She was hypervigilant as well, feeling unsafe and seeing others as potential threats to her personal safety. Not only could she not concentrate in class, but she had little motivation to do so. She was worried about her younger siblings and missed her mother. Her preoccupations made it difficult to attend to what was happening in class. Furthermore, she was generally tired and could muster little energy to struggle with academics.

Sometimes Tami tried to do her work, usually when she found it fairly easy, such as math problems. On occasion, she frantically wrote down random answers so the assignment looked complete. Other times, she simply gave up, seeming to be unable to handle the additional bit of stress that was produced. This happened most frequently when the assignments required writing or when Tami realized that she had no idea how to even begin an assignment, because she could not understand the directions. Her mind often went blank when she was anxious, resulting in her disoriented look. In addition, Tami dreaded tests, which seemed to drain her. Because Tami had essentially "missed" more than half of the school year, she did not have the skills she needed to progress to the next grade.

AGGRESSION AND ANTISOCIAL BEHAVIOR

Aggression and antisocial behavior have often been linked to poor school outcomes. Specifically, Cornwall and Bawden's (1992) critical review of cross-sectional research, follow-up, and longitudinal studies led the authors to assert that such behavior worsens schools performance, which leads to overall academic underachievement and less desirable life outcomes. For example, truancy, negative attitudes toward school, and failure to complete assignments make it difficult for a student's cognitive skills to be strengthened. This exaggerates any initial deficits and affects the student's overall level of mastery of material. Antisocial behavior problems have also been found to decrease attachment to and involvement in academics (Williams & McGee, 1994). If students with dyslexia have not been able to acquire basic reading skills and have become accustomed to acting out to avoid school, their delinquency may become a significant barrier to accessing appropriate remedial services. For example, suspensions from school will reduce their overall learning time and contribute to school personnel's negative attitudes toward them. Not only do the students' original learning problems go unresolved, but they fall further and further behind their peers. The following case study shows how disruptive behavior can significantly hamper a child's learning and achievement.

❖ CASE STUDY: The Disruptive Child

Juan was in sixth grade, but he could have easily passed for a much older child. Not only was he taller and more physically mature than his peers, but his overall demeanor seemed older as well. Juan was a tough kid, which his teachers had attributed to his rough home situation and personal circumstances. As the eldest child, his immigrant parents seemed to place a great deal of responsibility on his shoulders—almost too much, as he was expected to serve as the family translator and work at his father's landscaping business after school and on weekends. In addition, Juan had a chronic medical condition—juvenile diabetes—which he was primarily responsible for managing, as his parents did not seem to comprehend how to help.

Juan seemed ill at ease in school, only appearing comfortable when he was with his friends, who were generally considered to be the school "troublemakers." Together, their acting-out behaviors had progressed over the years to include more serious violations, such as ganging up on younger children, initiating physical fights, and even setting small fires in wastepaper baskets. Most of the time, when Juan's name was raised, it was in the context of a behavioral problem. In fact, many school personnel were completely unaware of Juan's significant math disability. Even as a sixth grader, Juan needed to count on his fingers to do simple arithmetic. He did not comprehend the functions of multiplication or division, let alone begin to understand how to approach word problems. His resource room teacher had long grown weary of trying to track him down before class and to try to motivate him to work on his basic skills. On some days, she didn't even bother looking for him. In the meantime, Juan was falling further behind his classmates and was increasingly eager not to let the differences show. His disruptive behaviors often landed him in the principal's office, where he sat for hours doing absolutely nothing.

The middle-school teachers had already heard about Juan and his serious behavior problems. In fact, one teacher even stated that he would refuse to allow Juan to be assigned to his classroom, because he "already had too many like him." Similar to most of his elementary school teachers, the middle-school teachers were much less aware of Juan's tremendous need for remedial services. Consequently, they were poised to perpetuate Juan's cycle of underutilization of services.

Juan's behavior problems overshadowed his academic needs. His math abilities had suffered in part because his acting-out behaviors reduced his class time. Not only did he miss out on lessons that he could have done well on, but the holes in his understanding prevented him from mastering new material. Juan's math aversion also weakened his motivation to attempt any math activities and further lowered his frustration tolerance for his struggle with math. In addition, his inappropriate behavior alienated him from his teachers and others who might have been able to help. It is possible that Juan could proceed through his schooling without any measurable improvement in his math abilities. As a result, he would not only lack basic computational skills but also applied math skills, which could interfere with his future employment potential.

PROVIDING SUPPORT

Regardless of the specific issue, all students with learning disabilities and emotional problems can benefit from extra encouragement throughout the school day. In particular, providing a bit of reassurance and some additional attention during difficult lessons or assignments may enable a child to persevere rather than give up.

A quick but extremely effective way of doing this is to use Encouragement Cards. Simple sentiments, such as "Keep trying" and "I'm proud of you" can be printed on colorful cards (or you can use the ones at the end of this chapter). Whenever you perceive that a child may need some encouragement, place a card on his or her desk. You can do this without having to interrupt your train of thought or breaking your stride during a lesson. Students appreciate the special attention, particularly because it feels like a secret between the two of you. Also, because it is in a sense nonverbal and tangible, you are more likely to have an impact, whereas you may be ignored if you only say the same message. You can expand these cards to suit your individual style and classroom. For example, after reading your students the story of *Simon and the Big Tree* (found at the end of this chapter), you might use a visual image to reinforce your encouragement and give out "Snail Cards" that remind your students of the story and its lesson of perseverance. Stickers such as small stars can also be quickly stuck onto a student's paper (or better yet, their hand) for a special bit of encouragement. If you do use stickers, however, be sure to use them only for providing encouragement and not as a reinforcer for actual achievement.

It is important to find creative ways to provide emotional support for your individual students. Janet Hart, a gifted and innovative fourth-grade teacher, recounts her experience with a unique 11-year-old boy who was learning disabled:

> This very challenging student came from a silent home where both parents were completely deaf. . . . My first task was to undo the learned behavior of "not listening" when a student or teacher was speaking. . . . I needed to find a way to connect with him outside of the regular classroom setting which seemed noisy and overwhelming to him because of how it contrasted to his very silent home life. I asked him what made him happy, and he said, "The times when I sit with my grandmother and have tea with her in pretty flowered cups." Because our room was across the hall from the Life Skills room, I was able to recreate that environment for him. During our first of many after school "homework clubs" (i.e., he never turned in any homework so it was all done after school), we went to the classroom kitchen and found tea cups, complete with flowers, made two cups of tea and took them back to our room.
>
> Once the student was free of the normal classroom distractions and in a setting that seemed familiar and safe, we also were able to break down some of the learning barriers that were holding him back. He slowly began to write short complete sentences, expressing his own ideas and seeing for himself that he truly had something important to contribute to whatever it was that the class was studying.

Though it may not be possible to share a flowered tea cup with every student, the times when such a special breakthrough is made are tremendously rewarding. Using your personal relationship with students can go a long way toward enabling them to overcome emotional problems and concentrate on learning.

Other ways to decrease the likelihood that emotional problems will exacerbate learning disabilities include (a) establishing a supportive classroom climate that makes risk taking and making mistakes safe and (b) providing a quiet space for children to take a brief break or regroup their energy during a challenging task. These and other interventions are discussed more fully in Chapter 7 on promoting emotional and psychological well-being.

SUMMARY

Emotional problems can intensify learning disabilities by interfering with learning. Negative patterns of coping, such as through avoidance or passivity and external locus of control, prevent children from investing themselves in tackling their learning struggles. Emotional disorders, such as depression and anxiety, also reduce achievement by interfering with children's thinking and memory. Low self-esteem can contribute to a self-fulfilling prophecy of failure. Aggression and antisocial behavior have also been found to be associated with poor performance by creating barriers to learning. Intervention focused on providing emotional support and promoting emotional health are important for each of these areas of emotional functioning.

BUILDING COPING SKILLS

Rest and Regroup

Count to 10; first forward, then backward. Let your mind rest as you are going forward and focus your attention on the task as you count backward.

Positive Self-Talk

Remind yourself of your successes. Tell yourself you can work hard to get past the difficult problem you face.

Ask for Help

Figure out what kind of help you need—explaining directions, suggestions for what to write, help reading new words, etc.—and then ask the person who will most likely be able to help you with it.

Reward Yourself

After doing something well or finishing something difficult, reward yourself with something special, like some treats you have brought from home.

Start Over

If you get stuck in the middle of a problem, start over again. Trying a new approach may help you do it right this time.

Talk to Someone

If you're feeling upset, tell someone before you get too worked up to do anything. Don't let your feelings get in the way of your accomplishments.

Easy-Hard

For difficult assignments, take turns doing something easy and something hard, such as doing an easy question and then a hard one.

Break It Up

Turn a big task into lots of little ones. Concentrate on completing one little part at a time before doing the next one. Pretty soon the whole thing will be done.

Relax

Imagine a calm scene and take some deep breaths. You can do it.

ENCOURAGEMENT CARDS

You can do it!	*I'm impressed.*
Calm yourself.	*Don't give up!*
Keep trying.	*I'm proud of you.*
Good effort.	*You're almost there.*

Story Time: Simon and the Big Tree

Simon the Snail lived in Mrs. Whitmore's garden with lots of other creatures. Each had its own home, but Simon, always wanting to improve on his home, decided he wanted to have a nice tree in front of his house for shade. He knew exactly which one he wanted—a big palm tree in a beautiful pot that Mrs. Whitmore had placed at the front of the garden.

As Simon set out from his house at the back of the garden to the palm tree, he was greeted by Wendy the Songbird.

"Good morning, Simon," she sang. "What are you doing today?"

Simon replied excitedly, "Hello, Wendy! I'm going to move the palm tree in front of my house so I can have some shade."

Wendy laughed. "You, move a tree?! Why, you're just a snail! You can't move a big tree like that!"

With a flutter of her wings, Wendy was gone, laughing so loud that it woke up Timmy the Turtle.

"What's Wendy laughing about," he asked.

"She thinks I can't move the palm tree in front of my house," Simon replied.

"Huh, huh, huh," Timmy chuckled slowly. "No wonder. Of course you can't. You're too small and weak."

"I can," cried Simon, "I'll show you."

Simon got to the potted palm tree and started to push. He pushed and pushed with all his might, but the tree wouldn't move. Simon began to feel sad. "Maybe they're right," he thought. "Maybe I can't do this after all." By now it was past noon, and the hot sun shone so brightly that Simon had to rest under the shade of the tree. "Oh my," he thought, "how I would like to have this cool shade in front of my house." Simon thought and thought while he sat under the tree. Suddenly, he had an idea. He would go see his friend Rachel the Raccoon.

"Rachel," he asked, "can you help me do something special?"

"You know I'll always help you, Simon. What is it?" she said with a smile.

"I want to move the palm tree in front of my house so I can have some shade," Simon began, "but I need your help."

"Oh Simon," Rachel sighed. "I'm not strong enough to do that by myself."

"We'll do it together and it'll be easy," Simon exclaimed excitedly. "I have a plan."

Simon and Rachel waited until it was just past dusk, when the ground was cool and a bit of dew was starting to form. Then as fast as he could, Simon went back and forth from the tree to his house, leaving an extra thick trail of slime behind him. When he was finished, there was a slippery path, just wide enough for the beautiful potted tree. "Now!" cried Simon. Rachel began to push. A few shoves with her body against the side of the pot and off it went! The potted palm tree slid down the slippery path that Simon had made, straight to Simon's door.

"Hurray," shouted Simon, "good teamwork, Rachel!"

She replied, "No, good thinking, Simon!"

EMOTIONAL HEALTH ENHANCES LEARNING

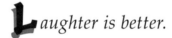

Laughter is better.

—Adele Phyllis Unterberg
Art teacher
29 years of teaching experience
New York, New York

Traditionally, the majority of attention given to learning and emotional problems has centered on the negative interaction of the two. This is certainly significant, since each can have profound effects on the other. Equally, if not more important, however, is the fact that emotional health can facilitate learning and serve as a buffer against the negative consequences of having learning disabilities.

If you reflect on your own experience, you will no doubt find examples of the importance of a positive emotional state when you are trying to accomplish something. Feeling happy and contented typically coincides with being open to new things, feeling creative, and having the energy to be productive. Mistakes may be quickly brushed aside or laughed off, and challenges can be approached with fervor. Excitement about learning something new may decrease self-consciousness and enable you to take risks that you might not otherwise have taken (e.g., possibly embarrassing yourself when you agree to be a volunteer on stage). Feeling that you can meet a challenge may give you extra persistence, whereas otherwise you might have given up hope and abandoned effort.

Children seem to be just as, if not even more, directly affected by their emotional states. Developmental stages for children are often described with regard to their emotions—think of the "terrible twos," the "clingy" 3-year-old, the "angelic" 5-year-old, as well as the "moody" teenager. In part, this may be because children spend less energy trying to hide their emotions than adults, and they display them for all to see. In addition, these emotions are central to their development and growth.

As teachers of elementary-aged children, it is particularly important to recognize the profound role of emotions in the classroom. Not only do the overall climate of the classroom and attitude of the teacher affect children's learning and achievement, but specific areas of emotional health that will facilitate learning can be fostered.

CLASSROOM CLIMATE

The climate of the school refers not only to the physical environment but also to the more intangible emotional and psychological experiences of being part of the school. On one extreme, a school may have very few financial resources and may be struggling just to have adequate heating. Classroom supplies may be limited, and books may be old or outdated. Staff may be overwhelmed, and students may be preoccupied with other life circumstances. It is reasonable that children who live in and are attempting to learn in this type of environment may have little motivation to devote themselves to school. On the other extreme, schools benefiting from substantial funding and solid parental involvement may have brightly painted and decorated halls and rooms as well as modern technological equipment and supplies. Children and staff alike may be excited to enter school, which they see as pleasant and conducive to creative expression and exploration.

The overall school climate has been found to have a significant impact on the adjustment, academic competence, and achievement of children in kindergarten through second grade (Esposito, 1999). Furthermore, the school climate "contributes almost as much as the child's own history of adjustment to how well parents perceive their children to be currently doing in school" (Esposito,

1999, p. 375). As teachers, you sometimes have little control over the overall school climate. However, the classroom climate is an important part of the overall school climate. Students watch their teachers far more closely than they attend to the school in general. You can focus on your own classroom environment, knowing that this will have a significant impact on your students.

The emotional and psychological climate of the classroom can range from dreary and sparse to bright and energizing. Elements that make up the emotional/psychological climate of the classroom include the quality of teacher-student relationships, teacher fairness toward students, teacher availability and students' ease of accessing help, emotional expression in the classroom, and teacher attitudes toward students. (Students also contribute a great deal to the climate of the classroom. However, since their contributions are not under the control of the teacher, they will not be emphasized here.) In their extremes, teacher-student relationships can be characterized by understanding, patience, a sense of humor, and affection, or they can be quite hostile, demanding, and intolerant. Teachers may see themselves as nurturing young minds or as overworked, underpaid babysitters of unruly children. Some classrooms are places where laughter is often heard; others are bastions of criticism and frustration. Certainly, every teacher has good and bad days, and even the most understanding and caring teacher can snap at a student. Adele Unterberg, who inspires her urban students to create amazing works of art, shares this anecdote:

> One day, I was so tired and stressed out, that I thought I would collapse in front of my class. The children were becoming very noisy during a particular project. I began to raise my voice and shout, "Silence, silence! I must have silence! My head is splitting."
>
> One little girl burst out laughing and said, "You're so funny, Ms. Unterberg." The class followed and laughed along. I felt so ashamed of my shouting that I calmed down and thanked her. The lesson continued, and the noise quieted. I was amazed that the children thought I was funny—I really was not—but it turned out very well after all.

Your overall attitude and pattern of behavior set the tone for the classroom and are what children come to expect at the start of each day. These expectations are important because they determine if children approach the classroom with dread or anticipation.

Taking the time to ensure a positive classroom climate is worth the effort. Not only will students respond better, but you will also find that the day is more enjoyable for you. Classroom meetings are one way to create a positive climate for learning and relationship building, because they build communication and facilitate an accepting, reflective environment (Zimmet & Friedman, 1999). Instructions for implementing a classroom meeting can be found in The Class Meeting activity sheet at the end of this chapter. A much more informal (but perhaps more frequent) "chat time," lasting a few minutes in duration, can also be implemented for the same purpose. This may entail taking a few minutes to casually talk with students about how they are experiencing the school day, or it can focus on problem solving for a specific issue.

Little actions throughout the day also affect the classroom climate. For example, you should approach praise and encouragement with the same intensity and effort as you would discipline. If you interrupt a class lesson or activity to tell a child to return to his or her seat or otherwise chastise a child, you should also interrupt the class to point out a child's achievement or something positive about the class. Small kindnesses, such as saying "please" and "thank you," should be expected of both students *and* teachers. Other ideas for creating a positive classroom climate can be found in the Creating a Positive Classroom Climate activity sheet at the end of this chapter.

POSITIVE MOOD

The importance of positive mood cannot be overestimated. Research on the impact of positive mood on physical health suggests that it provides resilience and makes personal resources more accessible (Salovey, Rothman, Detweiler, & Steward, 2000). In addition, positive mood has even been found to boost the body's immune system, suggesting that its impact extends beyond emotional states to physiological changes (Salovey et al., 2000). Positive mood has been found to enhance memory, cognitive flexibility, and creative problem solving (Bryan, Mathur, & Sullivan, 1996). Furthermore, research has shown that children with learning disabilities have more accurate computational skills (Bryan & Bryan, 1991) and short-term memory (Yasutake & Bryan, 1995) when in a positive mood than when in a neutral mood. Even more compelling research has shown that children with learning disabilities outperformed their nondisabled peers (who were in a neutral mood) on novel language-learning tasks when they had a positive mood (Bryan et al., 1996). This continued to be true even on reexamination 2 weeks later, suggesting that the effects of positive mood were not limited to initial learning. Instead, it may have affected more global processes such as cognitive organization and memory for long-term learning effects.

What constitutes a positive mood? It is unique to each individual and consequently can be created by the children themselves. Significant results have been found by simply encouraging students to think of something happy for 30 seconds to 2 minutes (Bryan et al., 1996). Cartoons, movies, stories, and games have all been used to induce positive moods (Bryan et al., 1996). This is perhaps one of the quickest, easiest, and most successful interventions a teacher can use to facilitate learning. Creating an overall positive classroom climate is important, because it increases the likelihood that an individual child will experience a positive mood. One teacher greeted her sixth-grade students with the following notice on the classroom door:

> This bright new day, complete with 24 hours of opportunities, choices and attitudes . . . [is] a perfectly matched set of 1,440 minutes. This unique gift, this one day, cannot be exchanged or refunded. Handle with care. Make the most of it. There is only one to a customer.

In addition to sharing inspirational quotes, you can induce positive mood in your students in a variety of ways. Consider this creative activity suggested by Marilyn Iverson, a special education teacher in Renton, Washington:

Year after year, boys and girls, no matter the age—they love the ritual. I tell my students the story that Fairy Dust is gathered by the Good Fairy. The Good Fairy gathers a pinch of Love, a pinch of Hope, a pinch of Luck, and a pinch of Kindness. She magically mixes them all together to make Fairy Dust. Fairy Dust must be used with Love and Hope in your heart.

When my students have a birthday, I give them a small velvet pouch (old jewelry pouches work great) and I sprinkle some Fairy Dust (fine glitter) into the pouch. As I sprinkle the Fairy Dust, I say, "A pinch in your pocket, a pinch in your shoe. Something good will happen to you!"

My students know that they must tie up the pouch and not take it out of their pocket until they reach home and can put it into a safe place. We seem to get what we expect out of life. Fairy Dust helps them to accept the positive.

Additional suggestions for generating positive mood in students can be found in the Inducing Positive Moods activity sheet at the end of this chapter.

EMOTIONAL EXPRESSION

Appropriate emotional expression is essential to overall emotional and psychological health and has a strong impact on both learning and personal experiences in school. Being unable to control your emotions can be a disturbing experience, and it often has negative consequences for relationships. The opposite, stifling your emotions or allowing them to build up without any release, can be overwhelming and taxing. Both approaches leave little energy for learning. Consequently, teaching your students to express their emotions verbally so they do not build up is helpful for both internalizing and externalizing disorders. Appropriate emotional expression also ensures that the child will be able to solicit needed support from others.

Appropriate emotional expression means being able to experience emotions and communicate them to others in a controlled manner. Venting that leads to decreased emotional intensity is productive, whereas getting more agitated as a result is not. Established curricula for teaching appropriate emotional expression provide comprehensive models of instruction. In addition, you can facilitate appropriate emotional expression in a variety of ways. Perhaps most important is modeling. Teachers are people too, and they experience frustration, joy, disappointment, anger, and contentedness just as anyone else would. Being aware of your own emotional state and sharing it appropriately with students not only provides a good example of emotional well-being but can be a powerful intervention tool. Of course, this does not mean you should yell, "You drive me crazy," though you might feel just that. It does mean sensitively conveying your disappointment when a child chooses to mistreat a peer. This teaches children to share their emotions with others, because their actions affect those around them. As a side benefit, the genuineness of your feelings may result in greater behavioral change than harsh reprimanding or punishment.

Appropriate expression of emotions can increase a child's frustration tolerance and decrease the likelihood of acting out. For example, when children encounter a task that they feel is beyond their ability, they may become exasperated and be tempted to give up. Openly recognizing their frustration and validating it as normal, given the circumstances, diffuses some of the energy behind the frustration. As a result, children may be more willing to persevere. (Think of your own experiences of waiting in line for a long time. When the inconvenience is acknowledged and your frustration validated, it often seems easier to wait.)

You can also facilitate healthy emotional expression by teaching feelings vocabulary, so that children have multiple words to more accurately convey their feelings. Rather than saying they feel "mad" about everything, teach them to recognize when they feel "disappointed" and "overwhelmed." You can use these words as extra credit items on spelling or vocabulary tests or incorporate them into a lesson on synonyms and antonyms. As a time-filler (such as when you are waiting to go to lunch), have the class generate as many words as possible related to a certain emotion. Visual aids, such as posters showing different faces and emotions, are also helpful. For example, *ABC Feelings* (by Alexandra Delis-Abrams, Ph.D.) has pictures of emotions for each letter of the alphabet, such as "J-jealous." In addition to giving children labels for emotions, point out real-life examples of how people handle emotions and discuss them with the class. Point out consequences for inappropriate expression and benefits for dealing with emotions well. Role playing, or playing charades using emotions, can also make these lessons more concrete. A child can act out a feeling and have others guess what it is. Clues can be provided as well, such as describing a situation that might result in the feeling being acted. Be sure to supervise this activity so you can ensure that the demonstrations are appropriate. A list of feeling words that can be used in various activities can be found on the Feeling Words reproducible at the end of this chapter. Having children's books that teach children about emotions is also useful. Selected books and materials I have found to be particularly worthwhile are listed in the annotated bibliography in Resource B.

ACCOMMODATING TEMPERAMENT

The concept of temperament is often used in describing the need to treat each child as an individual. The definition of temperament is not entirely consistent among researchers but typically refers to an inborn "behavioral style, the characteristic way that the individual experiences and responds to the internal and external environment" (Carey, 1998, p. 523). Some of the aspects that comprise temperament are adaptability/flexibility, persistence, approach/withdrawal, emotional regulation, and attention span. Each child has a unique temperament, and "individual differences in temperament mean that the 'same' environment will be processed differently by different children" (Rothbart & Jones, 1998, p. 484). Most individuals can adjust to accommodate their environment. Sometimes, however, there is a "temperament mismatch." Your own temperament may clash with your student's, or your expectations of what a "good student" is may be temperament-based (e.g., good students are calm and quiet). Being able to work around this fundamental difference is crucial to addressing the child's needs and avoiding excessive frustration on your part.

Certain behaviors of children may not be abnormal but may reflect overall temperament (Carey, 1998). For example, a child with a "difficult" temperament may be moody, very intense, and have difficulty adapting to changes and others' expectations in his or her environment. This may be difficult to tolerate on a daily basis, and teachers need to be able to distance themselves from the disturbing behavior by recognizing that it is part of the child's behavioral style rather than intentionally disruptive behavior (Carey, 1998). Failing to manage this temperamental variation may result in behavioral problems in the child that interfere with the learning process. In addition, this may lead to the child developing a coping style that is oppositional and even less resistant to intervention, not to mention endless frustration for you.

On the other end of the spectrum is a child who is temperamentally shy and resistant to novelty, who may not initiate interaction with peers or engage in active exploration (Henderson & Fox, 1998). This limits both social and academic growth. Accommodating temperament does not mean that you have to bend over backward to tolerate and excuse students' behaviors. Rather, it refers to the need to be aware of how temperamental differences may be interfering with a child's learning and to adjust your teaching accordingly. For example, how readily a child engages in classroom tasks is in part a function of temperamental differences in reacting to the unfamiliar (Henderson & Fox, 1998). Shy children can be encouraged to participate more openly when teachers use more personal comments and positive acknowledgments rather than frequent questions (Evans & Bienert, 1992). A child whose temperament is characterized by a low sensory threshold and withdrawal will need particular encouragement to engage in self-directed activities. This may mean encouraging the child not to hide during center time but to join one other student in a quiet reading task.

The ultimate goal is to help children overcome the temperamental traits that interfere with their personal and social growth and learning. In the process, teacher distress should be reduced, and the unpleasant struggle that previously may have characterized a relationship with a student should become more neutral or pleasant (McClowry, 1998). Furthermore, shaping temperament traits to be more conducive to positive reactions from others (e.g., willingness to help) has been found to guard against future negative outcomes (Werner, 1993). Suggestions for addressing common temperament traits can be found on the Accommodating Temperament Traits Ideas activity sheet at the end of this chapter.

INCREASING SENSE OF CONTROL

Research has shown that many children with learning disabilities have an external locus of control (Halmhuber & Paris, 1993; Rogers & Saklofske, 1985). These children have difficulty seeing how they influence their own success and failure and may attribute their achievement to factors outside themselves, such as luck or task difficulty. External locus of control can lead to feelings of hopelessness and the abandonment of effort. Conversely, having a sense that you can influence the outcomes of your actions can lead to greater motivation to take risks and to persist, despite obstacles. Building a child's sense of control requires more than simply telling a child that they are in control of their learning. Feeling like you have some degree of control usually means you feel you can take action and affect a situation. Equipping children with problem-solving strategies and response options reduces passivity.

One way to encourage problem solving is to refrain from immediately solving a student's problem. Rather than jumping in with a suggestion or solution, you will be more helpful if you guide the students with questions. You might ask them to tell you what solutions they are considering and help them evaluate the solutions by asking about the benefits or drawbacks of each. Helping children to think in this way builds the sense that they can tackle situations that are difficult. Consider this common dialog about a writing assignment:

Student: I don't know how to do this.

Teacher: Read the directions.

Student: I did. I don't get it.

Teacher: Just pick a person you admire and pretend you're writing a letter to him or her. You can ask them what their hobbies are, if they like their job, anything you want to know about them.

Instead, you could encourage problem solving and a sense of control with the following alternative response:

Student: I don't know how to do this.

Teacher: Tell me what you understand about it.

Student: I'm supposed to write a letter.

Teacher: Right, to whom?

Student: Someone I think is interesting.

Teacher: Right.

Student: But what am I supposed to write?

Teacher: There are lots of things you can write. Have you ever written a letter to a friend?

Student: Yeah.

Teacher: What did you write?

Student: I told him about my birthday party.

Teacher: Anything else?

Student: I asked him what he got for Christmas.

Teacher: Good. So there were at least two types of things you wrote— you asked questions about things you wanted to know about him and you told him some things about yourself. This is the same thing, but since you've never met the person you're writing to, you'll have even more to ask and tell. Does that make sense?

Student: Yeah, I get it.

Teacher: See, you know how to write a great letter.

Obviously, the second approach took more time. However, in that scenario, the student was left with a sense that he already knew how to do the assignment and could do it well, rather than doubting his abilities. Although the second approach may initially seem more time consuming, it actually is not, if you consider the high probability that the child in the first scenario is likely to raise his hand after writing two questions to ask, "Now what?"

BUILDING SELF-ESTEEM

Problems with self-esteem can hinder achievement through self-fulfilling prophecy. Conversely, a solid sense of personal worth can enhance learning by increasing the motivation to do well and by building perseverance and a willingness to take risks. The importance of raising children's self-esteem has become increasingly acknowledged by schools, so that entire programs are adopted. Even without a formal program, however, you can make a significant impact on self-esteem by encouraging positive affect and hopeful expectation (Hiebert, Wong, & Hunter, 1982). For example, rather than allowing a child to think or say, "I can't do this" or "I'm too stupid to learn this," you can help students use positive coping statements such as "I can learn how to do this" and "Even though it's hard, I can try my best." Meichenbaum's (1977) self-instructional techniques are particularly helpful in changing children's self-verbalizations. He encourages beginning with self-observation, or becoming aware of self-defeating internal dialogue. This may be the tiny voice inside that says, "You'll make a fool of yourself if you try that," and prevents you from taking risks. Changing that dialogue requires acquiring new skills so that you have the necessary abilities to succeed and actively altering your mind-set to be more adaptive and positive.

Increasing children's sense of self-esteem is intricately related to making them aware of their special worth as unique individuals. Stories are an excellent way to communicate this, such as those found in the annotated bibliography in Resource B. A child's self-concept and self-esteem can also be built by providing positive reinforcement and personal encouragement. In the case study that follows, a teacher describes her experience helping a child with a reading disability during her training (adapted from Cheng Gorman, 1999).

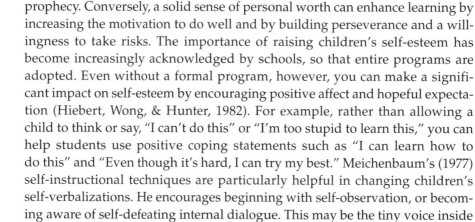

✧ CASE STUDY: The Hopeful Student

I couldn't help but notice Shalema when I entered the second-grade classroom where I was to do my student teaching practicum. She sat in the back row, barely fitting into her chair and towering over the other students. When I asked about her, my master teacher told me that Shalema "barely had the reading skills of a kindergartner," but because of her size, was promoted to the second grade. For most of the day, Shalema sat staring into space and twirling her hair. She was never disruptive, but she also never participated in class activities and didn't have any friends.

My master teacher tried to give her individual attention, but because there were 30 other students, Shalema didn't get much one-on-one time. I was happy when I was asked to work individually with Shalema, since she was so sweet, but I really didn't know what to expect from a second grader, or what to do.

We started by reading a preprimer book she had. Shalema was pretty uncomfortable about reading with me. When she actually read the word *is,* I got excited. I told her how proud I was of her for trying so hard and even told her that she could read well (which I believed, since I didn't really know what reading abilities to expect from a second grader). Shalema began to look forward to her times with me and became eager to read the few sight words she knew. In fact, sometimes she would excitedly scan the page and point out all the sight words she knew before she would start "reading" it. Of her own accord, she also began to take out her preprimer books during reading period and read to herself.

One day, Shalema's mother came to class and reported that Shalema had asked her to buy books to read at home, and they had been sitting down after dinner each night to read. She couldn't believe her daughter's change in attitude and gleefully reported that Shalema had read her first book. I was so encouraged, I announced to the class that Shalema had made "great progress." Much to my surprise, the class responded by spontaneously giving her thunderous applause. I'll never forget Shalema's smile that day.

Shalema struggled to catch up to her peers and continued to have difficulty reading. Her change in self-perception, however, as well as the positive feedback from her teacher and classmates, increased Shalema's desire to learn to read. She eagerly participated in remedial reading sessions and regularly sought out her teacher to show her the progress she had made.

ASSERTIVENESS AND SELF-ADVOCACY

Helping children to take initiative and responsibility for their learning and growth is an essential part of the emotional and psychological education that teachers provide. This requires self-confidence, assertiveness, and tenacity and is appropriate for children of all ages. Even very young children can be taught to seek help appropriately, to remind others of their special needs and accommodations, and to be proactive rather than to passively wait for assistance.

Assertive behavior is defined as expressing one's "feelings, attitudes, wishes, opinions or rights directly, firmly, and honestly, while respecting the feelings, attitudes, wishes, opinions and rights of the other person(s)" (Alberti et al., 1976). It is essential for children to acquire assertiveness skills early in order to decrease the passivity that impedes development and may be associated with adult psychopathology (Michelson, Sugai, Wood, & Kazdin, 1983). It is also helpful for children to be able to distinguish between assertive and aggressive behavior as ways to meet their needs. Using descriptive images can help convey the differences between passive, assertive, and aggressive behavioral styles. For example, passivity can be described as a "timid mouse," aggression as an "attacking lion," and assertiveness as a "confident stallion."

In the classroom, assertiveness is the foundation for such essential skills as requesting help, contributing to discussion, asking a question, making friends, expressing feelings appropriately, and responding to teasing and/or bullying (McGinnis & Goldstein, 1984). In addition, it has positive repercussions for the child's personal development and growth. Being able to assertively approach an adult or peer with a request for help provides children with a sense of control over their learning. It also has great impact on social relationships, which in turn affect learning. One group of teachers decided to begin assertiveness "clubs" for their fifth- and sixth-grade girls, whom they perceived as succumbing to peer pressure and "dumbing down" (e.g., pretending not to know answers in order to flirt with boys). Assertiveness also serves as a buffer against the long-term emotional and psychological ramifications of having learning disabilities, since self-reliance is of increasing importance as the child matures. Equipping children with skills to advocate for their own needs can have long-lasting benefits beyond the classroom.

DEALING WITH FAILURE

The ability to handle failure is an often overlooked aspect of emotional health. Everyone has faults and areas of insecurity, and everyone makes mistakes. Not being able to tolerate these failings may result in a child avoiding anything that seems risky or difficult. For example, 9-year-old Marcus was exceptionally bright but had an extremely difficult time acknowledging his weaknesses. If others corrected him in any way, he would immediately become defensive and withdraw from the interaction or activity. Marcus also shied away from activities that would challenge his abilities and consequently did not make the most of his intelligence.

To maximize the learning process, you have to take risks and stretch beyond your present abilities. If children are able to deal well with failure, it is likely that they will not become incapacitated by the learning struggles they will continue to face throughout their life. One way to help children live with their limitations and to grow from their failures is to promote self-acceptance. The Mistake of the Week classroom activity sheet teaches a healthy approach to failure. (A full description of this activity and reproducible for classroom use can be found at the end of this chapter.) It can also be helpful to teach children to find the silver lining in their experiences of failure, so that they begin to view them as part of their learning and development rather than feel shame about their failures.

RESILIENCE

Resilience is the ability to succeed despite obstacles and challenging circumstances (Garmezy & Masten, 1991). Since it is inevitable that children with learning disabilities and/or emotional disorders will face numerous challenges, building resilience is especially important. Researchers have found that healthy self-esteem and the understanding of one's learning disability as circumscribed serve as protective factors for individuals with learning disabilities (Morrison & Cosden, 1997). Actively fostering these areas, such as by using interventions discussed here and in Chapter 6, will naturally build your students' resilience.

Other factors that encourage resilience are faith that problems can be overcome, supportive adults who can be trusted, and realistic educational expectations (Werner, 1993). The vehicle for these factors is your relationship with your students. Believing in your students, being excited for their futures, and communicating your caring (not only to that student but also to others about that student) are likely to instill the same feelings in your students. Other suggestions for building resilience include identifying and reinforcing "islands of competence," such as by allowing students to showcase their talents, and enabling your students to make a contribution to the school milieu, perhaps by tutoring younger students (Brooks, 1994).

Last, good verbal ability and academic achievement have also been linked to positive life outcomes (Masten & Coatsworth, 1998), which reiterates the need to invest in a child's learning and achievement as ways to nurture their emotional well-being.

SUMMARY

Emotional well-being enhances learning in a variety of ways. Creating a positive classroom environment, inducing positive mood, and promoting a learning mind-set all enable your students to tackle challenges and help them feel good about themselves. In addition, fostering healthy emotional expression and an internal locus of control will build your students' internal resources. Gently adjusting temperament traits that might interfere with learning is also helpful. Last, helping your students deal with failure in a constructive manner and teaching them to be advocates for themselves will foster resilience.

CLASSROOM ACTIVITY:
THE CLASS MEETING

RATIONALE:

Conducting a class meeting is an excellent way to discuss any issues affecting the class as a whole. Such meetings help build an atmosphere of caring, cooperation, and collective identity. In addition, by involving students in group discussion and decision making, it is more likely that they will be invested in the outcomes of the meeting.

Examples of when to use a class meeting include dealing with group behavioral or social issues, preparing students for a change in the class or school, introducing a new classroom policy, and brainstorming on a problem affecting the majority of the class.

HOW TO:

Prepare students by informing them of a specific time that the class meeting will take place. State what issue will be addressed (limit it to one only) and what the goal(s) of the meeting will be (e.g., to find solutions to a problem, to discuss feelings, etc.). Reinforce this by posting a notice or writing the information on the chalkboard.

At the outset of the meeting, remind students of the parameters of the discussion and of the need for each comment or suggestion to be treated with respect. Also remind them of any time frame for the discussion, so that you are able to pace the discussion and reach any decisions or conclusions prior to its ending. Restate the issue and elicit thoughts from students prior to sharing your own opinions. When concluding the meeting, provide a summary of the discussion and ask students for their feedback (e.g., "Does the issue seem settled, or do we need to talk more?"). If a decision or outcome has been reached, note this and write it on the posted notice or chalkboard for reinforcement. Remember to praise students for their contributions, thoughtfulness, patience with and respect for one another, and mature participation.

CAVEATS:

Do not use the class meeting as a forum for chastising students. Certainly there may be a time when the entire class must be addressed and disciplined as a whole. However, the class meeting should be reserved for two-way communication and problem solving. If it is used as the teacher's soapbox, future honest participation from the students will be discouraged. It is also counterproductive in establishing a positive emotional climate.

CREATING A POSITIVE CLASSROOM CLIMATE

Accentuate the positive. Take a minute each day to point out a student's accomplishments to the entire class, even if it is as seemingly insignificant as noting that a child remembered to bring his or her books to school.

Be intolerant of negativity. Whether it is a child being mean to a peer or someone making a discouraging comment, don't let it pass without stopping to explain why such behavior is counterproductive and hurtful to everyone.

Encourage appropriate help-seeking. Reinforce children for knowing their limits and seeking assistance appropriately, such as by asking for specific help from the right sources.

Discourage passivity. If a task is too difficult or overwhelming, encourage students to break it up into smaller manageable parts.

Foster problem solving. When students say they are unable to do something, ask what solutions they have tried before intervening.

Model self-acceptance. If you make a mistake, admit it and use it as an opportunity to model honesty, tolerance for each other, and a willingness to learn from your mistakes.

Make each student feel special. Take a moment during the week to recognize a student's unique talents and qualities by privately expressing appreciation for them in a brief one-on-one.

Be interested in students' lives outside the school day. Children love to tell about themselves and need to know you have the time to listen to them.

Help students accept their failures as well as their successes. Students should be able to honestly acknowledge both.

Value spontaneity. Every now and then, a spontaneous fun moment, such as a minute spent making "raspberries" at each other, takes the monotony out of the day and communicates that you are together to learn and have fun too.

Teach forgiveness. Emphasizing the need to accept each other, faults and all, is more realistic than always having to make things "fair."

INDUCING POSITIVE MOODS

What to say:

"Think of something that makes you happy."

"Pretend a special friend is sitting next to you."

"Imagine yourself getting a special prize for doing well."

"Remember something you did really well and are proud of."

"Imagine yourself getting a standing ovation for getting the top score on this test."

"Close your eyes and think of something you enjoy."

What to do:

Sing a silly song that makes the children laugh.

Invite a few students to share jokes with the class.

Tell students something funny about yourself.

Have a laugh fest—the entire class laughs for 1 to 2 minutes.

Provide genuine praise for something the class has accomplished.

See who can make a comical face.

Inform students of any special incentives for their performance.

Use guided imagery to motivate students (e.g., climbing a mountain and reaching the top).

Remind students of a special activity or holiday coming up soon.

Show students a humorous cartoon or drawing.

FEELING WORDS

MAD

angry

frustrated

upset

embarrassed

irritable

jealous

disgusted

SAD

disappointed

discouraged

thoughtful

depressed

guilty

confused

lonely

HAPPY

excited

satisfied

pleased

silly

dreamy

proud

confident

SCARED

worried

stressed

shocked

surprised

overwhelmed

frightened

anxious

ACCOMMODATING TEMPERAMENT TRAITS

Negative Mood:

- Recognize the warning signs of impending or worsening mood change.
- Use positive mood inducers at the first sign of a mood change.
- Teach coping skills, such as relaxation training and talking to others.
- Build the child's awareness of the impact of their mood on learning and relationships.

Inflexibility:

- Be patient and give a little time for the child to adjust.
- Warn the child of impending change.
- Slowly build up to the change in small increments.
- Talk about the child's anxieties and concerns before the change.
- Give some sense of control in decision making, however small.
- Provide reassurance that the change will be good.

Intense emotional outbursts:

- Use time-outs and encourage the use of self-imposed time-outs.
- Teach more appropriate expression via direct instruction (role plays) and modeling.
- Ignore what is not too disruptive and teach peers to do the same.
- Model restraint.
- Identify early indicators of outbursts to proactively divert them.
- Reinforce and praise emotional control.

Sensory overload:

- Provide "quiet times" such as through brief solitary activities.
- Monitor the overall energy level of the classroom and the child's immediate environment for excessive noise and activity.
- Teach children to close their eyes and do relaxation exercises as needed.
- Encourage interaction with one or two peers at a time.

Shyness:

- Allow some time for the child to become comfortable in a situation before engaging them in an activity (e.g., calling on other students first).

- Provide reassurance.

- Suggest simple social gestures like smiling at a neighbor.

- Use positive comments (e.g., "You are writing well") rather than questions (e.g., "What are you writing?") to elicit interaction.

- Encourage the child to approach you when they are ready, rather than always going to them.

Giving up easily:

- Break tasks into smaller manageable components.

- Use frequent positive reinforcement for a successful completion of task components.

- Teach the child to look at sections or parts of assignments rather than the whole assignment.

- Provide tangible aids (e.g., help organizing an assignment) at the outset of the task.

- Teach the use of positive self-talk (e.g., "Two down, three to go!").

Easily overexcited:

- Provide early prompts to calm down.

- Give suggestions for the appropriate release of pent-up energy (e.g., running as fast as the child can for 3 minutes during the beginning of recess).

- Direct the child to a quiet place in the classroom as needed.

- Stay near the child for activities that might be too overstimulating (e.g., a classroom visitor).

CLASSROOM ACTIVITY: MISTAKE OF THE WEEK

RATIONALE:

This activity is designed primarily to promote appropriate acceptance of personal limitations and to help students learn from their mistakes. It has the added benefit of contributing to a supportive positive classroom climate and modeling honesty and openness. It is recommended as a weekly activity, at least initially, until the tone and procedure are firmly established. It can then be used as a monthly or periodic activity.

When first implementing this activity, the teacher should model all aspects of the activity, rather than choosing a student. It is very important to set the appropriate tone for the activity and to discourage teasing and other undesirable interactions. When it seems that students understand the activity, student submissions can be solicited, and one or two can be chosen for the class presentation and discussion. You can choose to limit the mistakes to academic or subject matter or include other areas as well. For example, interpersonal "mistakes" such as demonstrating poor judgment, mistreating a peer, or exhibiting socially inappropriate behavior can all be used. "Procedural" mistakes, those that involve the class schedule, task directions, and class or school rules can also be used.

HOW TO:

Throughout the week, the Learning From My Mistakes form (Worksheet 7.1) should be accessible to students (e.g., in a folder or as a center activity). When instructed to or on their own initiative, students should use the form to identify what mistake was made and why it occurred. More important, they should specifically state what they learned from it and how the mistake can be avoided in the future. The completed forms should be placed in an specific envelope or box (a "confidential" receptacle) and should be reviewed by the teacher prior to the activity.

On the day of the activity, the teacher should pick one or two mistakes to be shared with the class. Ideally, these are mistakes that are common to other students or particularly valuable learning experiences. The chosen students should be encouraged to share their mistakes with the class, and some brief discussion should occur (e.g., "Has anyone else made this mistake?" and "What other ways can the mistake be avoided?"). Last, the child(ren) who presented should be reinforced and praised for learning from their mistakes and having the courage to share them with others. This step must occur, and your praise should be as specific as possible.

The tone of the activity should be fun. You can make it more enjoyable by treating it like a television talk show featuring your "special guests," complete with a microphone (a foam ball on a pencil works well) and applause from the audience. You might even consider giving "prizes" (e.g., certificates or fancy erasers) or somehow recognizing the student in a special way (e.g., first in line for lunch).

CAVEATS:

This activity should be approached very thoughtfully, because it has the potential of being a negative experience. This activity is limited by your own comfort level with your mistakes. To provide the proper atmosphere of acceptance (rather than condemnation or attention for undesirable behavior), you must recognize the value of accepting yourself, faults and all. Ideally, every student would be asked to contribute to the weekly pile of forms to discourage teasing. Peers should not be permitted to say anything demeaning (e.g., "Only a baby would make that mistake!"). Such comments should be dealt with firmly by noting that everyone makes mistakes and it takes more courage to share mistakes than to hide behind them.

VARIATIONS:

Numerous variations for this activity can be made to accommodate the response of your class. For example, if, despite your best efforts, the classroom atmosphere does not permit supportive group sharing, you can use this as a private activity (e.g., an end-of-the-week assignment that is not shared aloud). If this is the case, be sure to provide positive feedback to each student. You may want to begin using the activity for a particular subject, such as math, to reinforce new skills and expand it to other areas if the students seem to enjoy the activity. You can also extend it to personal "mistake logs" or students' personal collections of their Learning From My Mistakes forms. You can refer to these personal records if you notice the student committing a similar error.

LEARNING FROM MY MISTAKES

Name: Date:

The mistake I made was . . .

I figured out I made a mistake because . . .

What I learned from my mistake was . . .

In the future, I can avoid this mistake by . . .

RESOURCE A:

ADDITIONAL RESOURCES

EMOTIONAL AND BEHAVIORAL PROBLEMS

A.D.D. WareHouse (materials for educators)
300 N.W. 70th Avenue
Plantation, FL 33317
(800) 233-9273

Children and Adults with Attention Deficit Disorder (C.H.A.D.D.)
        (information & support groups)
499 N.W. 70th Avenue
Plantation, FL 33317
(305) 587-3700

Conflict Resolutions Resources for Schools and Youth (resources for educators)
The Community Board Program
1540 Market Street, Room 490
San Francisco, CA 94102
(415) 552-1250

Council for Children with Behavioral Disorders
        (on-line catalog and legislation updates)
(888) CEC-SPED
www.ccbd.net

LEARNING DISABILITIES

Council for Exceptional Children (training opportunities and legislation
    updates)
1920 Association Drive
Reston, VA 20191
(888) CEC-SPED
www.cec.spec.org

Educational Resources Information Center Clearinghouse on Disabilities and
    Gifted Children (information and referrals; materials for educators)
Council for Exceptional Children
1920 Association Drive
Reston, VA 22091
(800) 328-0272

International Dyslexia Association (information for adults and children with
    dyslexia)
    (formerly the Orton Dyslexia Society)
Chester Building, Suite 380
8600 LaSalle Road
Baltimore, MD 21286
(800) ABCD-123
www.interdys.org

Learning Disabilities Network (educational and support services)
72 Sharp Street, Suite A-2
Hingham, MA 02043
(617) 340-5605

Selected Texts for Additional Learning

Brophy, J. (1996). *Teaching problem students.* New York: Guilford.
    Presents research and wise counsel on working with difficult students.

Lerner, J. (1993). *Learning disabilities: Theories, diagnosis & teaching strategies.*
    Boston: Houghton Mifflin.
    Comprehensive text on learning disabilities, including many references to teaching
    methods.

McGinnis, E., & Goldstein, A. P. (1984). *Skillstreaming the elementary school child:*
    A guide for teaching prosocial skills. Champaign, IL: Research Press.
    Provides teaching modules for specific social skills.

Novick, B. Z., & Arnold, M. M. (1995). *Why is my child having trouble at school?*
    New York: Putnam.
    Discusses core learning abilities and how to seek professional help for learning
    disabilities.

O'Shea, L. J., O'Shea, D. J., & Algozzine, B. (1998). *Learning disabilities: From*
    theory toward practice. Upper Saddle River, NJ: Merrill.
    Introductory text presents theory and practical classroom applications.

RESOURCE B:

ANNOTATED BIBLIOGRAPHY OF CHILDREN'S BOOKS AND MATERIALS

FEELINGS

ABC Feelings, by Alexandra Delis-Abrams, Ph.D.
> *Coloring books and a multicultural poster use illustrations of children in various situations to depict emotions that range from A-ccepted to Z-ippy.*
> *These can be purchased from Western Psychological Services by telephone (800-648-8857) or online (www.wpspublish.com).*

Andrew's Angry Words, by Dorothy Lachner
> *When Andrew gets angry and shouts a bunch of hurtful words, he learns the importance of expressing anger appropriately.*

Don't Rant and Rave on Wednesdays, by Adolph Moser, Ed.D.
> *In a humorous yet informative manner, this book shows children how to reduce the anger they feel and control their behavior.*

"How are you feeling today?" (illustrated by Jim Borgman)
> *A poster (in English or Spanish) asks, "How are you feeling today?" and has 30 amusing cartoons of facial expressions accompanying emotions such as "confident" and "surprised." A smaller version is magnetic and can be placed on a file cabinet for the teacher to let her students know how she's feeling!*
> *These can be purchased from Western Psychological Services by telephone (800-648-8857) or online (www.wpspublish.com).*

The Jester Has Lost His Jingle, by David Saltzman
> *The jester sets off on a quest to find laughter and learns it is within himself.*

Sometimes I Feel Like a Mouse, by Jeanne Modesitt
This simple and beautifully illustrated book pairs a feeling with an animal, such as a roaring lion, to depict anger.

The Very Angry Day That Amy Didn't Have, by Lawrence Shapiro, Ph.D.
Margaret and Amy both are having very bad days, but Margaret makes her day worse with her angry reactions. This book helps illustrate the impact our actions have on our emotions.

SELF-ESTEEM

Don't Feed the Monster on Tuesdays, by Adolph Moser, Ed.D.
This book teaches children not to "feed the monster" inside us that makes us feel bad about ourselves, and explains techniques such as positive self-talk.

Odd Velvet, by Mary E. Whitcomb
A little girl who doesn't seem to fit in reminds her classmates that she isn't so different after all.

Ready-To-Use Self-Esteem Activities for Young Children, by Jean R. Feldman
This sourcebook of activities helps teachers (and parents) build self-esteem in children aged 8 and up.

The Lovables, by Diane Loomans
Twenty-four animals live in the Kingdom of Self-Esteem, where each has a unique contribution to make.

You Are Special, by Max Lucado
Punicello learns that knowing he is loved for who he is makes the mean things other people say matter little.

SOCIAL ISOLATION

Nobody Likes Me, by Raoul Krischanitz
The new dog in town is lonely but gives up at the slightest hint of rejection. He learns how to make friends by taking risks.

Somebody Loves You, Mr. Hatch, by Eileen Spinelli
Mr. Hatch is a lonely man who keeps to himself until he receives a mysterious valentine that teaches him that when he allows others to see who he really is, he really does have friends.

REFERENCES

Abrams, J. C. (1986). On learning disabilities: Affective considerations. *Journal of Reading, Writing and Learning Disabilities, 2,* 189-196.

Alberti, R., Emmons, M., Fodor, I., Galassi, J., Galassi, M., Jakubowski, P., & Wolfe, J. (1976, November). *Ethical principles and guidelines for assertiveness training learners and groups.* Paper presented at the meeting of the Association for Advancement of Behavior Therapy, New York.

Alyward, G. P. (1985). Understanding and treatment of childhood depression. *Journal of Pediatrics, 107*(1), 1-9.

American Psychiatric Association. (1994). *Diagnostic and statistical manual of mental disorders* (4th ed.). Washington, DC: Author.

Azar, B. (2000). What's the link between speed and reading in children with dyslexia? *Monitor on Psychology, 31*(3), 36-39.

Baker, J. M., & Zigmond, N. (1990). Are regular education classes equipped to accommodate students with learning disabilities? *Exceptional Children, 56,* 515-526.

Baker, L., & Brown, A. L. (1984). Cognitive monitoring in reading. In J. Flood (Ed.), *Understanding reading comprehension* (pp. 21-44). Newark, DE: International Reading Association.

Bakker, D. J. (1992). Neuropsychological classification and treatment of dyslexia. *Journal of Learning Disabilities, 25*(2), 102-110.

Barga, N. K. (1996). Students with learning disabilities in education: Managing a disability. *Journal of Learning Disabilities, 29*(4), 413-421.

Barkley, R. A. (1990). *Attention-deficit/hyperactivity disorder: A handbook for diagnosis and treatment.* New York: Guilford.

Barrett, P. M., Rapee, R. M., Dadds, M. M., & Ryan, S. M. (1996). Family enhancement of cognitive style in anxious and aggressive children. *Journal of Abnormal Child Psychology, 24*(2), 187-203.

Bear, G. G., & Minke, K. M. (1996). Positive bias in maintenance of self-worth among children with LD. *Learning Disability Quarterly, 19,* 23-32.

Bender, W. N., Vail, C. O., & Scott, K. (1995). Teachers' attitudes toward increased mainstreaming: Implementing effective instruction for students with learning disabilities. *Journal of Learning Disabilities, 28*(2), 87-94.

Bender, W. N., & Wall, M. E. (1994). Social-emotional development of students with learning disabilities. *Learning Disability Quarterly, 17,* 323-341.

Benson, D. F., & Geschwind, N. (1970). Developmental Gerstmann syndrome. *Neurology, 20,* 293-298.

Bergin, C., & Bergin, D. A. (1999). Classroom discipline that promotes self-control. *Journal of Applied Developmental Psychology, 20*(2), 189-206.

Birmaher, B., Ryan, N., Williamson, D., Brent, D., Kaufman, J., Dahl, R., Perel, J., & Nelson, B. (1996). Childhood and adolescent depression: A review of the past 10 years, Part I. *Journal of the American Academy of Child and Adolescent Psychiatry, 35,* 1427-1439.

Borg, M. G., Riding, R. J., & Falzon, J. M. (1991). Stress in teaching: A study of occupational stress and its determinants, job satisfaction and career commitment among primary schoolteachers. *Educational Psychology, 11*(1), 59-75.

Bronson, M. B. (2000). *Self-regulation in early childhood: Nature & nurture.* New York: Guilford.

Brooks, R. B. (1994). Children at risk: Fostering resilience and hope. *American Journal of Orthopsychiatry, 64*(4), 545-553.

Brophy, J. (1986). Teacher influences on student achievement. *American Psychologist, 41,* 1069-1077.

Bruno, R. M. (1981). Interpretation of pictorially presented situations by learning disabled and normal children. *Journal of Learning Disabilities, 14,* 350-352.

Bryan, T., & Bryan, J. (1991). Positive mood and math performance. *Journal of Learning Disabilities, 24,* 490-494.

Bryan, T., Mathur, S., & Sullivan, K. (1996). The impact of positive mood on learning. *Learning Disability Quarterly, 19*(3), 153-162.

Bryan, T., & Nelson, C. (1994). Doing homework: Perspectives of elementary and junior high school students. *Journal of Learning Disabilities, 27,* 488-499.

Bryan, T. H. (1974). Peer popularity of learning disabled children. *Journal of Learning Disabilities, 7,* 621-625.

Bryan, T. H. (1977). Learning disabled children's comprehension of nonverbal communication. *Journal of Learning Disabilities, 10,* 36-41.

Cantwell, D. P., & Baker, L. (1991). Association between attention-deficit hyperactivity disorder and learning disorders. *Journal of Learning Disabilities, 24,* 88-95.

Carey, W. B. (1998). Temperament and behavior problems in the classroom. *School Psychology Review, 27*(4), 522-533.

Chadwick, O., Taylor, A., Heptinstall, E., & Danckaerts, M. (1999). Hyperactivity and reading disability: A longitudinal study of the nature of the association. *Journal of Child Psychology and Psychiatry, 40*(7), 1039-1050.

Chandler, L. A. (1994). Emotional aspects of learning problems: Implications for assessment. *Special Services in the Schools, 8*(2), 161-165.

Chapman, J. W. (1988). Learning disabled children's self-concepts. *Review of Educational Research, 58,* 347-371.

Cheng Gorman, J. (1999). Understanding children's hearts and minds: Emotional functioning and learning disabilities. *TEACHING Exceptional Children, 31*(3), 72-77.

Cicchetti, D., & Toth, S. L. (1998). The development of depression in children and adolescents. *American Psychologist, 53*(2), 221-241.

Clark, M. D. (1997). Teacher response to learning disability: A test of attributional principles. *Journal of Learning Disabilities, 30*(1), 69-79.

Coie, J. D., & Dodge, K. A. (1998). Aggression & antisocial behavior. In W. Damon (Series Ed.) & N. Eisenberg (Volume Ed.), *Handbook of child psychology: Vol. 3. Social, emotional & personality development* (5th ed., pp. 779-862). New York: Wiley.

Colvin, R. L. (1999, December 15). Learning: Many problems but many remedies. *Los Angeles Times,* p. B2.

Cornwall, A., & Bawden, H. N. (1992). Reading disabilities and aggression: A critical review. *Journal of Learning Disabilities, 25*(5), 281-288.

Crealock, C. M. (1986). Learning disabilities and the young offender: Exploration of causes of the relationship. In H. Stutt (Ed.), *Learning disabilities and the young offender: Arrest to disposition* (pp. 28-38). Ottawa, Canada: Canadian Association for Children and Adults with Learning Disabilities.

Dean, R. S., & Rattan, A. J. (1987). Measuring the effects of failure with learning disabled children. *International Journal of Neuroscience, 37,* 27-30.

Dodge, K. A. (1986). A social information processing model of social competence in children. In M. Perlmutter (Ed.), *Cognitive perspectives on children's social and behavioral development.* Hillsdale, NJ: Erlbaum.

Egan, G. J., Brown, R. T., Goonan, L., Goonan, B. T., & Celano, M. (1998). The development of decoding emotions in children with externalizing behavior disturbances and their normally developing peers. *Archives of Clinical Neuropsychology, 13*(4), 383-396.

Eisenberg, N., Fabes, R. A., Murphy, B. C., Shepard, S., Guthrie, I. K., Mazsk, P., Poulin, R., & Jones, S. (1999). Prediction of elementary school children's socially appropriate and problem behavior from anger reactions at age 4-6 years. *Journal of Applied Developmental Psychology, 20*(1), 119-142.

Elbaum, B. E., Schumm, J. S., & Vaughn, S. (1997). Urban middle-elementary students' perceptions of grouping formats for reading instruction. *Elementary School Journal, 97,* 475-500.

Esposito, C. (1999). Learning in urban blight: School climate and its effect on the school performance of urban, minority, low-income children. *School Psychology Review, 28*(3) 365-377.

Evans, M. A., & Bienert, H. (1992). Control and paradox in teacher conversations with shy children. *Canadian Journal of Behavioural Science, 24,* 502-516.

Farrington, D. P. (1995). The development of offending and antisocial behaviour from childhood: Key findings from the Cambridge Study in Delinquent Development. *Journal of Child Psychology and Psychiatry, 36,* 929-964.

Fisher, B. L., Allen, R., & Kose, G. (1996). The relationship between anxiety and problem-solving skills in children with and without learning disabilities. *Journal of Learning Disabilities, 29*(4), 439-446.

Fleischner, J. E., Garnett, K., & Shepherd, M. J. (1982). Proficiency in basic fact computation of learning disabled and nondisabled children. *Focus on Learning Problems in Mathematics, 4,* 47-55.

Fleischner, J. E., & Manheimer, M. A. (1997). Math interventions for students with learning disabilities: Myths and realities. *School Psychology Review, 26*(3), 397-413.

Fox, C. L. (1989). Peer perceptions of learning disabled children in the regular classroom. *Exceptional Children, 56,* 50-59.

Fristad, M. A., Topolosky, S., Weller, E. B., & Weller, R. A. (1992). Depression and learning disabilities in children. *Journal of Affective Disorders, 26,* 53-58.

Garmezy, N., & Masten, A. S. (1991). The protective role of competence indicators in children at risk. In E. M. Cummings, A. L. Greene, & K. H. Karraker (Eds.), *Life-span developmental psychology: Perspectives on stress and coping* (pp. 151-174). Hillsdale, NJ: Lawrence Erlbaum.

Gibbs, D. P., & Cooper, E. B. (1989). Prevalence of communication disorders in students with learning disabilities. *Journal of Learning Disabilities, 22*(1), 60-63.

Gjone, H., & Stevenson, J. (1997). The association between internalizing and externalizing behavior in childhood and early adolescence: Genetic or environmental common influences? *Journal of Abnormal Child Psychology, 25*(4), 277-286.

Gresham, F. M., Lane, K. L., MacMillan, D. L., & Bocian, K. M. (1999). Social and academic profiles of externalizing and internalizing groups: Risk factors for emotional and behavioral disorders. *Behavioral Disorders, 24*(3), 231-245.

Grolnick, W. S., & Ryan, R. M. (1990). Self-perceptions, motivation and adjustment in children with learning disabilities: A multiple group comparison study. *Journal of Learning Disabilities, 23*, 177-184.

Hagborg, W. J. (1996). Self-concept and middle-school students with learning disabilities: A comparison of scholastic competence subgroups. *Learning Disability Quarterly, 19*, 117-126.

Hall, C. W., & Haws, D. (1989). Depressive symptomatology in learning-disabled and nonlearning-disabled students. *Psychology in the Schools, 26*, 359-364.

Halmhuber, N. L., & Paris, S. G. (1993). Perceptions of competence and control and the use of coping strategies by children with disabilities. *Learning Disability Quarterly, 16*, 93-111.

Haney, P., & Durlak, J. A. (1998). Changing self-esteem in children and adolescents: A meta-analytic review. *Journal of Clinical Child Psychology, 27*(4), 423-433.

Harris, K. R. (1986). The effects of cognitive-behavior modification on private speech and task performance during problem solving among learning-disabled and normally achieving children. *Journal of Abnormal Child Psychology, 14*(1), 63-67.

Hayek, R. A. (1987). The teacher assistance team: A prereferral support system. *Focus on Exceptional Children, 20*(1), 1-7.

Heath, N. L. (1995). Distortion and deficit: Self-perceived versus actual academic competence in depressed and nondepressed children with and without learning disabilities. *Learning Disability Research & Practice, 10*(1), 2-10.

Heath, N. L., & Wiener, J. (1996). Depression and nonacademic self-perceptions in children with and without learning disabilities. *Learning Disability Quarterly, 19*, 34-44.

Henderson, H. A., & Fox, N. A. (1998). Inhibited and uninhibited children: Challenges in school settings. *School Psychology Review, 27*(4), 492-505.

Heyman, W. B. (1990). The self-perception of a learning disability and its relationship to academic self-concept and self-esteem. *Journal of Learning Disabilities, 23*(8), 472-475.

Hiebert, B., Wong, B., & Hunter, M. (1982). Affective influences on learning disabled adolescents. *Learning Disability Quarterly, 5*(4), 334-343.

Holder, H. B., & Kirkpatrick, S. W. (1991). Interpretation of emotion from facial expressions in children with and without learning disabilities. *Journal of Learning Disabilities, 24*, 170-177.

Hurford, D. P., Schaug, J. D., Bunce, L., Blaich, T., & Moore, K. (1994). Early identification of children at risk for reading disabilities. *Journal of Learning Disabilities, 27*(6), 371-382.

Janney, R. E., & Snell, M. E. (1996). How teachers use peer interactions to include students with moderate and severe disabilities in elementary general education classes. *Journal of the Association for Persons with Severe Handicaps, 21,* 72-80.

Juvonen, J., & Bear, G. (1992). Social adjustment of children with and without learning disabilities in integrated classrooms. *Journal of Educational Psychology, 84*(3), 322-330.

Kashani, J. H., Cantwell, D. P., Shekim, W. O., & Reid, J. C. (1982). Major depressive disorder in children admitted to an inpatient community mental health center. *American Journal of Psychiatry, 139,* 671-672.

Kauffman, J. (1993). Characteristics of emotional and behavioral disorders of children and youth. New York: Macmillan.

Kershner, J. R. (1990). Self-concept and IQ as predictors of remedial success in children with learning disabilities. *Journal of Learning Disabilities, 23*(6), 368-374.

Klingner, J. K., & Vaughn, S. (1999). Students' perceptions of instruction in inclusion classrooms: Implications for students with learning disabilities. *Exceptional Children, 66*(1), 23-37.

Klingner, J. K., Vaughn, S., Schumm, J. S., Cohen, P., & Forgan, J. (1998). Inclusion or pull-out: Which do students prefer? *Journal of Learning Disabilities, 31,* 148-158.

Kloomok, S., & Cosden, M. (1994). Self-concept in children with learning disabilities: The relationship between global self-concept, academic "discounting," nonacademic self-concept and perceived social support. *Learning Disability Quarterly, 17,* 140-153.

Kovacs, M. (1996). Presentation and course of major depressive disorder during childhood and later years of the life span. *Journal of the American Academy of Child and Adolescent Psychiatry, 35,* 705-715.

Kravetz, S., Faust, M., Lipshitz, S., & Shalhav, A. (1999). LD, interpersonal understanding, and social behavior in the classroom. *Journal of Learning Disabilities, 32*(3), 248-255.

LaGreca, A. M. (1981). Social behavior and social perception in learning disabled children: A review with implications for social skills training. *Journal of Pediatric Psychology, 6,* 395-416.

Lauer, R., Giordani, B., Boivin, M., Halle, H., Glasgow, B., Alessi, N., & Berent, S. (1994). Effects of depression on memory performance and metamemory in children. *Journal of the American Academy of Child and Adolescent Psychiatry, 33*(5), 679-685.

Leitenberg, H., Yost, L. W., & Carroll-Wilson, M. (1986). Negative cognitive errors in children: Questionnaire development, normative data, and comparisons between children with and without self-reported symptoms of depression, low self-esteem, and evaluation anxiety. *Journal of Consulting and Clinical Psychology, 54,* 528-536.

Lerner, J. (1993). *Learning disabilities: Theories, diagnosis, and teaching strategies.* Boston: Houghton Mifflin.

Loeber, R., & Stouthamer-Loeber, M. (1998). Development of juvenile aggression and violence: Some common misconceptions and controversies. *American Psychologist, 53*(2), 242-259.

Margalit, M., & Levin-Alyagon, M. (1994). Learning disability subtyping, loneliness, and classroom adjustment. *Learning Disability Quarterly, 17*(4), 297-310.

Margalit, M., & Raviv, A. (1984). LD students' expressions of anxiety in terms of minor somatic complains. *Journal of Learning Disabilities, 17*, 226-228.

Margalit, M., & Zak, I. (1984). Anxiety and self-concept of learning disabled children. *Journal of Learning Disabilities, 17*, 537-539.

Masten, A. S., & Coatsworth, J. D.(1998). The development of competence in favorable and unfavorable environments: Lessons from research on successful children. *American Psychologist, 53*, 205-220.

McCauley, E., Myers, K., Mitchell, J., Calderon, R., Schloredt, K., & Treder, R. (1993). Depression in young people: Initial presentation and clinical course. *Journal of the American Academy of Child and Adolescent Psychiatry, 32*, 714-722.

McClowry, S. G. (1998). The science and art of using temperament as the basis for intervention. *School Psychology Review, 27*(4), 551-563.

McGee, R., Williams, S., Share, D. L., Anderson, J., & Silva, P. A. (1986). The relationship between specific reading retardation, general reading backwardness and behavior problems in a large sample of Dunnedin boys: A longitudinal study from 5 to 11 years. *Journal of Child Psychology and Psychiatry, 27*, 597-610.

McGinnis, E., & Goldstein, A. P. (1984). *Skillstreaming the elementary school child: A guide for teaching prosocial skills.* Champaign, IL: Research Press.

McLeskey, J., Henry, D., & Axelrod, M. I. (1999). Inclusion of students with learning disabilities: An examination of data from reports to congress. *Exceptional Children, 66*(1), 55-66.

McLeskey, J., Henry, D., & Hodges, D. (1998). Inclusion: Where is it happening? *TEACHING Exceptional Children, 31*, 4-11.

Meichenbaum, D. (1977). *Cognitive behavior modification: An integrative approach.* New York: Plenum.

Meichenbaum, D. (1984). Teaching thinking: A cognitive behavioral perspective. In J. Sigal, S. Chipman, & R. Glaser (Eds.), *Thinking & learning skills* (Vol. 2). Hillsdale, NJ: Lawrence Erlbaum.

Mercer, C. D., King-Sears, P., & Mercer, A. R. (1990). Learning disabilities definition and criteria used by state education departments. *Learning Disability Quarterly, 13*, 141-152.

Meyer, A. (1983). Origins and prevention of emotional disorders among learning disabled children. *Topics in Learning and Learning Disabilities, 3*, 59-70.

Michelson, L., Sugai, D. P., Wood, R. P., & Kazdin, A. E. (1983). *Social skills assessment and training with children: An empirically based handbook.* New York: Plenum.

Montalvo, A., Bair, J. H., & Boor, M. (1995). Teachers' perceptions of occupational stress factors. *Psychological Reports, 76*, 846.

Morrison, G. M., & Cosden, M. A. (1997). Risk, resilience and adjustment of individuals with learning disabilities. *Learning Disability Quarterly, 20*(1), 43-60.

Myers, P., & Hammill, D. D. (1990). Learning disabilities. Austin, TX: PRO-ED.

Oliver, M. (December 8, 1999). John Larkin: Scat singer overcame stuttering. *Los Angeles Times*, p. A25.

O'Shea, L. J., O'Shea, D. J., & Algozzine, B. (1998). *Learning disabilities: From theory toward practice.* Upper Saddle River, NJ: Merrill.

Parril-Burnstein, M. (1981). *Problem solving and learning disabilities: An information processing approach.* New York: Grune & Stratton.

Patten, B. (1973). Visually-mediated thinking: A report on the case of Albert Einstein. *Journal of Learning Disabilities, 6,* 415-420.

Patterson, G. R., Debaryshe, B. D., & Ramsey, E. (1989). A developmental perspective on antisocial behavior. *American Psychologist, 44,* 329-335.

Peck, M. (1985). Crisis intervention treatment with chronically and acutely suicidal adolescents. In M. Peck, N. L. Farberow, & R. E. Litman (Eds.), *Youth Suicide* (pp. 112-122). New York: Springer.

Pennington, B. F. (1991). *Diagnosing learning disorders: A neuropsychological framework.* New York: Guilford.

Prout, H. T., Marcal, S. D., & Marcal, D. C. (1992). A meta-analysis of self-reported personality characteristics of children and adolescents with learning disabilities. *Journal of Psychoeducational Assessment, 10,* 59-64.

Rawson, H. E. (1992). The interrelationship of measures of manifest anxiety, self-esteem, locus of control, and depression in children with behavior problems. *Journal of Psychoeducational Assessment, 10,* 319-329.

Resnick, R. J. (2000). *The hidden disorder: A clinician's guide to attention deficit hyperactivity disorder in adults.* Washington, DC: American Psychological Association.

Reynolds, W. M. (1990). Depression in children and adolescents: Nature, diagnosis, assessment and treatment. *School Psychology Review, 19,* 158-173.

Richman, L. C., & Lindgren, S. D. (1981). Verbal mediation deficits: Relation to behavior and achievement in children. *Journal of Abnormal Psychology, 90*(2), 99-104.

Roberts, C., & Zubrick, S. (1993). Factors influencing the social status of children with mild academic disabilities in regular classrooms. *Exceptional Children, 59*(3), 192-202.

Rockefeller, N. (1976, October 16). *TV Guide,* pp. 12-14.

Rodriguez, C. M., & Routh, D. K. (1989). Depression, anxiety, and attributional style in learning-disabled and non-learning disabled children. *Journal of Clinical Child Psychology, 18,* 299-304.

Rogers, H., & Saklofske, D. H. (1985). Self-concepts, locus of control, and performance expectations of learning disabled children. *Journal of Learning Disabilities, 18,* 273-278.

Rothbart, M. K., & Jones, L. B. (1998). Temperament, self-regulation, and education. *School Psychology Review, 27*(4), 479-491.

Rothman, H. R., & Cosden, M. (1995). The relationship between self-perception of a learning disability and achievement, self-concept and social support. *Learning Disability Quarterly, 18,* 203-212.

Rourke, B. P., Young, G. C., & Leenaars, A. A. (1989). A childhood learning disability that predisposes those afflicted to adolescent and adult depression and suicide risk. *Journal of Learning Disabilities, 22*(3), 169-175.

Sabornie, E. J. (1994). Social-affective characteristics in early adolescents identified as learning disabled and nondisabled. *Learning Disability Quarterly, 17*(4), 268-279.

Sale, P. & Carey, O. M. (1995). The sociometric status of students with disabilities in a full-inclusion school. *Exceptional Children, 62,* 6-19.

Salovey, P., Rothman, A. J., Detweiler, J. B., & Steward, W. T. (2000). Emotional states and physical health. *American Psychologist, 55*(1), 110-121.

Schonhaut, S., & Satz, P. (1983). Prognosis for children with learning disabilities: A review of follow up studies. In M. Rutter (Ed.), *Developmental neuropsychiatry* (pp. 542-563). New York: Guilford.

Seguin, J. R., Boulerice, B., Harden, P. W., Tremblay, R. E., & Pihl, R. (1999). Executive functions and physical aggression after controlling for attention deficit hyperactivity disorder, general memory and IQ. *Journal of Child Psychology and Psychiatry, 40*(8), 1197-1208.

Seguin, J. R., Pihl, R. O., Harden, P. W., Tremblay, R. E., & Boulerice, B. (1995). Cognitive and neuropsychological characteristics of physically aggressive boys. *Journal of Abnormal Psychology, 104*(4), 614-624.

Sharma, S. (1970). Manifest anxiety and school achievement of adolescents. *Journal of Consulting and Clinical Psychology, 34*(3), 403-407.

Shaywitz, S. E. (1996, November). Dyslexia. *Scientific American.* pp. 98-104.

Shelton, T. L., & Barkley, R. A. (1995). The assessment and treatment of attention-deficit/hyperactivity disorder in children. In M. C. Roberts (Ed.), *Handbook of pediatric psychology,* New York: Guilford.

Sherif, M., Harvey, O. J., White, B. J., Hood, W. R., & Sherif, C. W. (1961). *Intergroup conflict and cooperation. The Robbers Cave Experiment.* Norman, OK: Institute of Group Relations.

Short, E. J. (1992). Cognitive, metacognitive, motivational, and affective differences among normally achieving, learning-disabled, and developmentally handicapped students: How much do they affect school achievement? *Journal of Clinical Child Psychology, 21*(3), 229-239.

Smith, D. D., & Luckasson, R. 1995). *Introduction to special education: Teaching in an age of challenge* (2nd ed.). Boston: Allyn & Bacon.

Spafford, C. S., & Grosser, G. S. (1993). The social misperception syndrome in children with learning disabilities: Social causes versus neurological variables. *Journal of Learning Disabilities, 26,* 178-198.

Stanley, P. D., Dai, Y., & Nolan, R. F. (1997). Differences in depression and self-esteem reported by learning disabled and behavior disordered middle school students. *Journal of Adolescence, 20,* 219-222.

Stevenson, D. T., & Romney, D. M. (1984). Depression in learning disabled children. *Journal of Learning Disabilities, 17,* 579-582.

Swanson, H. L., & Malone, S. (1992). Social skills and learning disabilities: A meta-analysis of the literature. *School Psychology Review, 21,* 427-443.

Taghavi, M. R., Neshat-Doost, H. T., Moradi, A. R., Yule, W., & Dalgleish, T. (1999). Biases in visual attention in children and adolescents with clinical anxiety and mixed anxiety-depression. *Journal of Abnormal Child Psychology, 27*(3), 215-223.

Tarnowski, K. J., & Nay, S. M. (1989). Loss of control in children with learning disabilities and hyperactivity: A subgroup analysis. *Journal of Learning Disabilities, 22,* 381-383.

Thompson, L. (1971). Language disabilities in men of eminence. *Journal of Learning Disabilities, 4,* 34-45.

Thompson, R. J., Lampron, L. B., Johnson, D. F., & Eckstein, T. L. (1990). Behavior problems in children with the presenting problem of poor school performance. *Journal of Pediatric Psychology, 15*(1), 3-20.

Tollefson, N., Tracy, D. B., Johnson, E. P., Buenning, M., Farmer, A., & Barke, C. R. (1982). Attribution patterns of learning disabled adolescents. *Learning Disability Quarterly, 5,* 14-20.

Tur-Kaspa, H., Weisel, A., & Segev, L. (1998). Attributions for feelings of loneliness of students with learning disabilities. *Learning Disabilities Research & Practice, 13*(2), 89-94.

U.S. Department of Education. (2000). *Twenty-first annual report to congress on the implementation of the Individuals with Disabilities Education Act.* Washington, DC: U.S. Department of Health, Education and Welfare.

U.S. Office of Education (1977, December 29). Education of handicapped children. *Assistance to the states: Procedures of evaluating specific learning disabilities.* (Federal Register, Part III). Washington, DC: U.S. Department of Health, Education, and Welfare.

Vaughn, S., Schumm, J. S., Klingner, J. K., & Saumell, L. (1995). Students' views of instructional practices: Implications for inclusion. *Learning Disability Quarterly, 18,* 236-248.

Vaughn, S., Schumm, J. S., Niarhos, F. J., & Gordon, J. (1993). Students' perceptions of two hypothetical teachers' instructional adaptations for low achievers. *Elementary School Journal, 94,* 87-103.

Vygotsky, L. (1978). *Mind in society: The development of higher psychological processes.* Cambridge, MA: Harvard University Press.

Ward, T. J., Ward, S. B., Glutting, J. J., & Hatt, C. V. (1999). Exceptional LD profile types for the WISC-III and WIAT. *School Psychology Review, 28*(4), 629-643.

Werner, E. E. (1993). Risk & resilience in individuals with learning disabilities: Lessons learned from the Kauai Longitudinal Study. *Learning Disabilities Research and Practice, 8,* 28-34.

Whitman, P. B., & Leitenberg, H. (1990). Negatively biased recall in children with self-reported symptoms of depression. *Journal of Abnormal Child Psychology, 18*(1), 15-27.

Williams, S., & McGee, R. (1994). Reading attainment and juvenile delinquency. *Journal of Child Psychology and Psychiatry, 35*(3), 441-459.

Wojnilower, D. A., & Gross, A. M. 1988). Knowledge, perception, and performance of assertive behavior in children with learning disabilities. *Journal of Learning Disabilities, 21,* 109-117.

Wong, B.Y.L., & Wong, R. (1980). Role taking skills in normal achieving and learning disabled children. *Learning Disability Quarterly, 3*(2), 11-17.

Wright-Strawderman, C., & Watson, B. L. (1992). The prevalence of depressive symptoms in children with learning disabilities. *Journal of Learning Disabilities, 25*(4), 258-264.

Yasutake, D., & Bryan, T. (1995). The influence of induced positive affect on middle school children with and without learning disabilities. *Learning Disabilities Research and Practice, 10,* 38-45.

Zimmet, M., & Friedman, H. (1999). *Enhancing children's social, emotional and academic development via classroom meetings: Another role for the school psychologist* (PC Report 7-99-15). New York: New York University, Psychoeducational Center.

INDEX

CORWIN
PRESS

The Corwin Press logo—a raven striding across an open book—represents the happy union of courage and learning. We are a professional-level publisher of books and journals for K–12 educators, and we are committed to creating and providing resources that embody these qualities. Corwin's motto is "Success for All Learners."